Counseling
American Muslims

Recent Titles in
Contributions in Psychology

Counseling the Inupiat Eskimo
Catherine Swan Reimer

Culturally Competent Family Therapy: A General Model
Shlomo Ariel

The Hyphenated American: The Hidden Injuries of Culture
John C. Papajohn

Brief Treatments for the Traumatized: A Project of the Green Cross
Foundation
Charles R. Figley, editor

Counseling Refugees: A Psychosocial Approach to Innovative
Multicultural Interventions
Fred Bemak, Rita Chi-Ying Chung, and Paul B. Pedersen

Health Related Counseling with Families of Diverse Cultures: Family,
Health, and Cultural Competencies
Ruth P. Cox

Acculturation and Psychological Adaptation
Vanessa Smith Castro

Progress in Asian Social Psychology: Conceptual and Empirical
Contributions
Kuo-Shu Yang, Kwang-Kuo Hwang, Paul B. Pedersen, Ikuo Daibo, editors

Vygotsky's and Leontiev's Holographic Semiotics and Psycholinguistics:
Applications for Education, Second Language Acquisition and Theories of
Language
Dorothy Robbins

The Arts in Contemporary Healing
Irma Dosamantes-Beaudry

The Politics of Stereotype: Psychology and Affirmative Action
Moises F. Salinas

Racial Sensitivity and Multicultural Training
Martin Strous

Counseling American Muslims

Understanding the Faith and Helping the People

AHMED NEZAR KOBEISY

Contributions in Psychology, Number 48
Paul Pedersen, Series Adviser

Westport, Connecticut
London

Library of Congress Cataloging-in-Publication Data

Kobeisy, Ahmed Nezar.
   Counseling American Muslims : understanding the faith and helping the people /
Ahmed Nezar Kobeisy.
        p.   cm. — (Contributions in psychology, ISSN 0736-2714 ; no. 48)
   Includes bibliographical references and index.
   ISBN 0-313-32472-7 (alk. paper)
      1. Muslims—Counseling of—United States.   2. Muslims—Mental health—United
   States.   3. Cross-cultural counseling—United States.   4. Islam—United States—
   Psychology.   5. United States—Ethnic relations—Psychological aspects.   6. Racism—
   United States—Psychological aspects.   I. Title.   II. Series.
   E184.M88K63   2004
   158'.3'088297—dc22   2004001332

British Library Cataloguing in Publication Data is available.

Library of Congress Catalog Card Number: 2004001332
ISBN: 0-313-32472-7
ISSN: 0736-2714

First published in 2004

Praeger Publishers, 88 Post Road West, Westport, CT 06881
An imprint of Greenwood Publishing Group, Inc.
www.praeger.com

Printed in the United States of America

∞

The paper used in this book complies with the
Permanent Paper Standard issued by the National
Information Standards Organization (Z39.48–1984).

10 9 8 7 6 5 4 3 2 1

Copyright Acknowledgment

Excerpts from *Islamic Values in the United States: A Comparative Study* by Yvonne Yazbeck
Haddad and Adair T. Lummis, copyright © 1987 by Oxford University Press, Inc. Used by
permission of Oxford University Press, Inc.

To the Souls of my first teachers, guides, role models, and mentors, my parents Muhammad Kobeisy and Aaminah Abd Allah.

May Allah (the Almighty God) bless their souls and bestow on them His eternal pleasure in the highest level of Paradise.

Contents

Series Foreword

Ahmed Kobeisy's volume promises to become the most important book published thus far in this series. It is important because the "American Experiment" in pluralistic democracy has never been in greater danger, and that danger relates directly to the global conflict between religions, cultures, and civilizations. In the necessary search for "homeland security," we are in danger of giving up the basic values articulated everywhere from the dollar bill to the Statue of Liberty, substituting simplistic stereotypes for the complexity of our culture and our culture's people, and being driven by our own fear and panic to impose forceful means of social change rather than free choice to accommodate both the similarities and differences in our society.

Kobeisy's book approaches this awesome task by emphasizing three different themes. The first theme is a documentation and recognition of complexity and diversity among Muslims and throughout Islam as a belief system. Psychology has been in danger of imposing a simplistic and stereotyped perspective of groups such as Muslims where there is a significant difference in contrast to the white, middle-class, urban male perspective without at the same time recognizing the many overlapping similarities between Islam and the other belief-defined groups in our society. Kobeisy does an excellent job of valuing both distinct differences and strategic similarities, thus connecting Islam to other belief-defined social systems.

The second theme is a factual and empirical documentation of Muslims as a rapidly growing population relative to other belief-defined groups in American society. This resource is especially important because there are so few published resources to set the record straight and to provide this factual/empirical documentation. As psychologists and particularly as counselors, we need to do our homework so that our decisions are based on fact rather than fiction. Both Muslim clients and their non-Muslim psychological service providers need this factual foundation as a shared starting point in their interaction. By introducing the reader to specific cases and examples of counseling Muslims, this book provides that foundation.

The third theme is that of discussing the implications for counselors to provide guidance and suggestions to counselors working with Muslim clients. Each suggestion and demonstration of developmental structures within Islam could assist the counselor in providing counseling. At the same time, demonstrations of why and how the Muslim client might be reluctant to seek out counselors and counseling will help that counselor deal with the very natural resistance that is likely to occur.

In our post–September 11 society, the Muslim community has, as Kobeisy points out, faced the double jeopardy of the tragedy itself and also being blamed by others in our society for similarities they share with those who created that tragedy. Not only is this Muslim community now at risk in our society, but so is the heritage of political and personal freedom for which so many in our society have freely sacrificed their lives on the battlefield. On September 12, 2001, a valued colleague e-mailed me asking if I thought America will have learned something from that tragedy. At the time, I was so filled by nationalistic self-pity that I was not ready to hear anything about what we could learn. As a dominant society, we have much more experience in "teaching" and "leading" others, particularly other minority groups in our society. Kobeisy's book offers the opportunity and promise to "learn" something about other groups such as the Muslim community and at the same time about ourselves.

Kobeisy is careful to relate his book to the "multicultural competencies" that have emerged in American psychology and particularly in counseling. He points out that this book is not just about American Muslims but, more important, also about multiculturalism itself in our society. The problems and opportunities of counseling Muslims include the mandate that counseling be relevant and meaningful to all groups in our society. Kobeisy does not present an alternative framework for conventional counseling but rather seeks to strengthen conventional counseling by more accurately applying psychological principles meaningfully.

Paul Pedersen, Series Editor, Contributions in Psychology
University of Hawaii

Preface

This volume is long overdue. It is urgently needed to fill a vacuum in the counseling literature and to enhance practitioners' effectiveness in assisting their Muslim clients through these difficult times. In the aftermath of the tragic events of September 11, 2001, American Muslims became doubly victimized. In addition to the grief and shock, among other traumatic consequences, of the terrorists' attacks, American Muslims have been suffering from hate and hate-related crimes against their persons and institutions. The ability of American Muslims to cope with the stressors and demands of new challenges has been negatively impacted because of, among other things, the lack of availability of information on Muslims' values, practices, and cultures and how such information is utilized in the development of sensitivity and professionalism in mental health fields and settings.

Although this book focuses on American Muslims, it broadens the concepts and practical experiences of multicultural counseling. No doubt the American demographic structure is changing rapidly. In a few years or decades, it is expected that whites will no longer be the majority. The ranking of various minority groups with respect to population numbers will also change. The majority will, therefore, be from nonwhite, non-European backgrounds. The Muslim community in the United States is also changing rapidly. Being one of the fastest-growing communities and religions in the world and in the United States, Islam now has more adherents in the United States than Episcopalians and soon will outnumber the Jewish population—if it has not done so already.

American Muslims are culturally and religiously diverse. Therefore, by examining and uncovering the complex and intersecting issues of race, culture, religion, profession, education, age, acculturation, and so on and their influences on the identity development of American Muslims, this book provides professionals with the tools they need to become more capable and effective in helping Muslim clients from various cultural backgrounds and in a wide range of issues. Furthermore, this book can be helpful in understanding issues and concerns of populations that share with American Muslims values, cultural norms, and practices while they differ from Western worldviews and values. Therefore, the counseling approaches, methods, and strategies suggested in this book for counseling Muslims will be applicable, to a great extent, to these non-Western and/ or nonwesternized populations.

In addition to the primary beneficiaries of this book (i.e., academicians, teachers, anthropologists, multicultural curriculum developers, counselors, health and mental health professionals, and so on), members as well as spiritual leaders of the Muslim community will be able to understand and appreciate the counseling and mental health services and consequently overcome the stigma associated with such services. Although some Muslims may cite Islam as a reference when opposing counseling, issues like improving communication skills, learning of career opportunities, job placement, and training to meet the continuously changing demands of the job market are but a few of the noncontroversial issues that Muslims can agree on.

Utilization of counseling services will help Muslims improve their lives, plan their careers, and resolve inter- as well as intrapersonal conflicts, thus acquiring stronger feelings of belonging to the communities in which they live. Finally, the general population may benefit from this book and expand their knowledge and understanding of Muslims in the United States with the hope of reducing prejudice-based problems and hate crimes.

On the one hand, this book articulates the experience and the needs of Muslims in counseling. During this process, it analyzes the intersection of individual self with various factors that make up American Muslims' identity and perceptions of themselves as well as of others. These factors include, among others, individual, familial, religious, cultural, social, and political ones.

On the other hand, this book takes the mystery out of the counseling profession and introduces it to the American Muslim population. Through the positive encounters that some Muslim clients have experienced in counseling, this book shows when and how counseling can be of benefit to American Muslims.

The great and urgent need for understanding the American Muslim population and for delivery of better services to them motivated me to present this book as a contribution to both the Muslim community and the counseling profession. However, this book does not present an alternative framework for existing Western counseling approaches; rather, it helps professionals understand which approaches can work best with American Muslims and when and how, thus allowing them to build on their expertise and employ their knowledge and experience in selectively applying existing models to suit the needs of their clients.

In order to help the readers in assessing their understanding of Muslim cultures, their awareness of their own biases toward this population, and the sources of such biases, a survey, "Self-Assessment on Islam and Muslim Cultures," has been provided preceding chapter 1. Answers to the survey's questions are also provided. In this survey as well as later in the book, I briefly address the areas of competencies for effective counseling for the Muslim population using the widely accepted "Multicultural Counseling Competencies and Standards: A Call to the Profession" (Sue, Arredondo, & McDavis, 1992) only as a base for this discussion.

In this model, Sue et al. (1992) developed a 3 (Characteristics) × 3 (Dimensions) matrix in which most cultural understandings can be organized or developed. For example, the characteristics (a) counselor awareness of own assumptions, values, and biases; (b) understanding of the worldview of the culturally different; and (c) developing appropriate strategies and techniques would be each described as having three dimensions: (a) beliefs and attitudes, (b) knowledge, and (c) skills. Thus, nine competency areas are identified.

PERSONAL ACCOUNT

Having served the most diverse religious community in the United States (namely, American Muslims) as a spiritual leader for more than 15 years gave me the opportunity to interact with various cultures within the Muslim community on a daily basis. Closely working with and struggling to gain the trust of various ethnic and cultural segments of the Muslim community provided me with an insider's insight and understanding of the practical applications and cultural interpretations of Islam rather than relying only on textual ones.

More important, it has allowed me to observe invisible signs of suffering and unexpressed cries for help that members of the Muslim community have but are unable to share with others. American Muslims are undergoing unprecedented experiences as they negotiate the meaning and application of Islam in an environment that is not aware of Islamic practices, let alone recognizing them. As a result, they are also experiencing personal, familial, emotional, educational, and professional challenges as they have never before. Furthermore, Muslims of both immigrant and indigenous backgrounds are encountering, for the first time, diversity and pluralism among themselves as well as in society at large. Various counseling and mental health professionals can be of tremendous help for Muslims if adequately prepared and trained.

Being a professional counselor for Muslim community members and working among Muslims for more than nine years has made me aware of the devastating effects of the lack of and/or bad counseling, which many Muslims encounter on a daily basis in school counseling, community counseling, and mental health services and institutions. This firsthand experience in both religious and counseling settings with Muslims granted me the status of becoming the primary resource for professionals when dealing with Muslim and Arab clients.

It is through my encounters with both clients and counselors and out of great desire to be of help that I decided to make this book as a humble contribution to both the American Muslim community and the counseling professions. On the one hand, Muslims, like all other groups, can greatly benefit from counseling. On the other, counselors too can become more effective with Muslims by being more understanding and sensitive to American Muslims.

Acknowledgments

All Praise is due to Allah, whose blessings and guidance in life are beyond words. I pray that He continues to bestow guidance on me for the rest of my life.

I wish to thank my teacher and mentor Dr. Paul Pedersen for his encouragement, support, and guidance. His motivation is unforgettable.

I wish also to thank my teacher, mentor, and companion since childhood until this time, my brother Shaikh Wael Alsharief. I am indebted to him for life.

The sacrifice, support, and encouragement of my wife Amera are admirable.

The patience, understanding, support, and assistance of my children Sumayyah, Muhammad, Ebraheem, Aminah, and Mariah are remarkable. I pray that they grow as role models to benefit their societies and the world.

The advice, contributions, and support of Nivine Amr, a dear friend and supporter, has been remarkable.

I am also thankful to my clients and to the counselors who helped make this book possible. I wish them the best in life.

Dr. Suzan Wadley's passion for genuine understanding of others, particularly for Muslims, has been a strong motivator for this work. I am indebted to her for her support and encouragement.

Self-Assessment on Islam and Muslim Cultures

This assessment consists of two parts: Part I is made of multiple-choice questions and is aimed at examining the reader's knowledge of the Islamic beliefs, practices, history, and demography as well as the factors of attitude formation toward Muslims. Part II is a true/false questionnaire. It is intended to test the counselor's information about Islam, attitude toward Muslims, and understanding of biases when working with Muslim populations. Please take a moment to go through the survey and compare your answer to the answer sheet made available at the end of the survey.

Part I: Answer the following questions by selecting only one answer for each question. Correct answers are provided at the end of this questionnaire.

A. History, Beliefs, and Practices

1. Islam was founded in:
   a. The fifth century.
   b. The sixth century.
   c. Before Christianity.
   d. The 1500s.
   e. None of the above.

2. Muhammad represents to Muslims:
   a. A divine-human figure.
   b. Only an ordinary human like all others.
   c. A prophet of God who is a role model for humanity.
   d. All of the above.
   e. None of the above.

3. The holy book for Muslims is:
   a. Hilal.
   b. The Bible.
   c. The Koran (Qur'an).
   d. The Torah.

4. Islam Considers Jesus and Moses:
   a. Great and noble men but who had no inspiration from God.
   b. Great and noble men who were prophets of God.
   c. Unworthy historic figures.
   d. Jesus was the son of God while Moses was not.
   e. None of the above.

5. Muslims believe in:
   a. One God.
   b. No God.
   c. Many Gods.
   d. Jesus Christ as God.

6. In Islam, Allah is:
   a. The God for Muslims.
   b. The Muslim God.
   c. God for Muslims, Jews, and Christians.
   d. The same as Muhammad.
   e. All of the above.

7. Muslims' place of worship is called:
   a. Church.
   b. Mosque.
   c. Temple.
   d. Other.

8. Islamic fundamentals of faith include:
   a. The oneness of God.
   b. Life after death.
   c. All prophets and messengers of God.
   d. All scriptures of God.
   e. All of the above.

9. Muslims pray to the direction of:
   a. The sun.
   b. The moon.
   c. Jerusalem.
   d. Mecca, Arabia.
   e. None of the above.

10. To fulfill one of their religious obligations, Muslims pray:

    a. Five times a day.

    b. Only twice a day.

    c. Only once a week.

    d. As often as they can.

    e. None of the above.

11. The weekly Sabbath for Muslims occurs on:

    a. Any day of the week.

    b. Sunday.

    c. Saturday.

    d. Friday.

    e. Thursday.

12. Ramadan is:

    a. A historic figure in Islam.

    b. One of the prayers Muslims perform daily.

    c. The month in which Muslims fast during the year.

    d. The name of the Muslim calendar.

    e. Another Islamic ritual.

13. Muslims' pilgrimage to Mecca in Arabia is called:

    a. Hijra.

    b. Hegira.

    c. Hajj.

    d. Zakat.

    e. None of the above.

14. Charity is an Islamic obligation to be paid annually. Muslims know it as:

    a. Hajj.

    b. Zakat.

    c. Sawm.

    d. All of the above.

    e. None of the above.

B. Demography

15. The number of Muslims worldwide is estimated at:

    a. Several million.

    b. One billion.

    c. More than one billion.

    d. Less than 50 million.

    e. Two billion.

16. The largest Muslim population exists in:

    a. The Middle East.

    b. Africa.

    c. Asia.

    d. Europe.

    e. The Americas.

17. Indonesia is:

    a. The largest Muslim country in the world.

    b. The only Muslim country in Asia.

    c. The most diverse country in Asia.

    d. The poorest Muslim country in the world.

    e. None of the above.

18. Arabs are:

    a. Only Muslims.

    b. People who speak Arabic regardless of religion.

    c. People of the Middle East.

    d. All of the above.

    e. None of the above.

19. The number of American Muslims is estimated at:

    a. Fifty thousand.

    b. Two and a half million.

    c. Six to eight million.

    d. One million.

    e. None of the above.

20. The American Muslim community is made up of:

    a. Mostly Arab immigrants.

    b. Only African Americans.

    c. People of diverse racial, ethnic, and national origin backgrounds.

    d. Only refugees.

    e. None of the above.

21. The Nation of Islam is:

    a. The same as other Muslims.

    b. Different from mainstream Muslims.

    c. The American interpretation of Islam.

    d. All of the above.

    e. None of the above.

22. The majority sect within Islam is called:
    a. Sunni.
    b. Shiite.
    c. Black Muslims.
    d. Middle Eastern.
    e. All of the above.

23. The Shiite population represents:
    a. 35 percent of the total world Muslim population.
    b. 50 percent of the total world Muslim population.
    c. Approximately 15 percent of the total world Muslim population.
    d. Less than 5 percent of the total world Muslim population.
    e. None of the above.

24. American Muslims:
    a. Are religiously devout and understand Islam the same way.
    b. Vary in their understanding and practice of Islam.
    c. Are nonpracticing people.
    d. Are all from immigrant backgrounds.
    e. None of the above.

25. Muslims' immigration to the United States dates back to:
    a. The late twentieth century.
    b. After World War I.
    c. After World War II.
    d. African slavery.
    e. The late eighteenth and early nineteenth centuries.

C. Attitude Formation

26. My main sources of knowing about Islam are:
    a. Parents.
    b. Religious institutions and religious leaders.
    c. The media and political events.
    d. All of the above.
    e. None of the above.

27. The events of September 11, 2001, helped:
    a. Provide me with a good understanding of what Islam is and who the Muslims are.
    b. Prove that all Muslims hate America.
    c. Me to inquire more about Islam and ask more questions.
    d. Prove that Muslims must not be allowed to live in America.
    e. None of the above.

28. The study of Islam and Muslim cultures is important because:
    a. It helps understand terrorism and terrorists' tactics.
    b. It provides better understanding of the world for mutual cooperation.
    c. It is necessary for graduation.
    d. It is necessary for political correctness.
    e. All of the above.
29. Islam as a religion spread widely in the world through:
    a. Forceful conversion.
    b. Wars and conflicts.
    c. Trades and immigration.
    d. Holy war.
    e. None of the above.
30. Islamic civilization:
    a. Contributed greatly to the Europeans' renaissance and created new fields of knowledge.
    b. Damaged the world's resources and lives.
    c. Created more conflicts and wars.
    d. All of the above.
    e. None of the above.
31. American Muslims would benefit greatly if they:
    a. Converted to another religion.
    b. Assimilated to the American culture.
    c. Left the United States.
    d. All of the above.
    e. None of the above.
32. The Arab–Israeli conflict proved that:
    a. Arabs do not like Jews to live among them.
    b. Arabs do not like democracy.
    c. Muslims hate Jews because of religious animosity.
    d. All of the above.
    e. None of the above.
33. Muslim women dress differently because:
    a. Islam oppresses women.
    b. Muslim men force their women to dress that way.
    c. Muslim women are oppressed and cannot express their opinions.
    d. All of the above.
    e. None of the above.

34. American Muslims:

    a. Appreciate democracy and pluralism.

    b. Desire totalitarian dictatorships.

    c. Hope to impose their way of life on others.

    d. All of the above.

    e. None of the above.

35. The American Muslim attitudes toward colleagues and neighbors of other faiths are:

    a. Friendly and collegial.

    b. Unfriendly and suspicious.

    c. Hostile and antagonistic.

    d. Mixed and unclear.

    e. None of the above.

36. Muslim children are likely to suffer from:

    a. Child abuse from Muslim parents.

    b. Developmental problems due to parents' negligence.

    c. Violence and domestic abuse in their homes.

    d. All of the above.

    e. None of the above.

37. Counselors should:

    a. Advocate for religious accommodation for American Muslims.

    b. Not advocate for religious accommodation for American Muslims.

    c. Council American Muslims on how to hide their religious practices.

    d. Help American Muslims abandon their religious values and principles.

    e. None of the above.

38. Muslims' negative attitude toward counseling can be attributed to the following:

    a. Muslims are uncivilized and oppose any modern service.

    b. Muslims do not like to be helped by non-Muslims.

    c. Muslims do not accept Western practices of mental health.

    d. Most Muslims are not aware of the availability of counseling.

    e. All of the above.

39. When counseling Muslims, counselors should:

    a. Convince clients to adapt to new cultural values and trends.

    b. Convince clients to change their cultural practices and norms.

    c. Attempt to understand clients' cultural and value systems.

    d. All of the above.

    e. None of the above.

40. Islam can be described as:

    a. A major world religion.

    b. A cult.

    c. A monolithic religion and culture.

    d. An evil and violent religion.

    e. All of the above.

41. Muslims can be described as:

    a. Homogeneous religiously and culturally.

    b. Diverse culturally but homogeneous religiously.

    c. Diverse both religiously and culturally.

    d. Homogeneous culturally but diverse religiously.

42. Muslim women:

    a. Have many rights in Islam.

    b. Have no rights in Islam.

    c. Have rights in Islam less than other cultures.

    d. Are the cause of men's problems.

    e. None of the above.

43. Terrorism in the world is:

    a. A Middle Eastern creation that must be stopped by force.

    b. The Arab cultural norm and must be stopped.

    c. Caused by Islam, and Muslims must reinterpret their religion in more peaceful ways.

    d. A world phenomenon that warrants the world's attention.

    e. None of the above.

44. I welcome having a Muslim as:

    a. A friend.

    b. A doctor.

    c. A governor of my state.

    d. All of the above.

    e. None of the above.

45. In the Islamic tradition, the term *jihad* refers mainly to:
    a. Holy war.
    b. Killing infidels.
    c. Struggle in all aspects of life, including combating when it is necessary.
    d. None of the above.

Part II:

No	Statement	True	False
1.	One of my sources on Islam and Muslims has been from the media	___	___
2.	One of my sources on Islam and Muslims has been from schools	___	___
3.	One of my sources on Islam and Muslims has been religious institutions	___	___
4.	One of my sources on Islam and Muslims has been my parents, relatives and friends	___	___
5.	One of my sources on Islam and Muslims has been from peers	___	___
6.	I have heard negative comments about Islam and Muslims from television	___	___
7.	I have read negative information about Islam and Muslims in books	___	___
8.	From my religious or spiritual leader, I have learned that Islam is not a good religion	___	___
9.	From my teachers, I have learned that Muslims are not trustworthy	___	___

10.	From my parent(s), I have heard negative comments on Islam and Muslims	___	___
11.	Most Muslims are from the Arab world	___	___
12.	I can identify Muslims by the way they look	___	___
13.	Islam oppresses women	___	___
14.	The media coverage of Islam has been mostly accurate	___	___
15.	Jihad gives legitimacy to killing people of different faiths.	___	___
16.	Islam condones terrorism.	___	___
17.	Islam forces its beliefs on others	___	___
18.	Muslims seek to dominate the world	___	___
19.	I would not elect a Muslim for public office	___	___
20.	I would not want to have a Muslim neighbor	___	___
21.	I would not let my children sleep over at their friend's house if they are Muslims	___	___
22	I have all the knowledge and experience needed to work effectively with Muslim clients	___	___
23	I should set the goals for my Muslim clients	___	___

24	I should help accelerate Muslim clients' integration into the society	——	——
25	I should counsel Muslim women to gain their freedom and independence from their husbands	——	——
26	Muslim clients should follow the advice of their counselors	——	——
27	Islam has a negative effect on the mental well being of Muslim clients	——	——
28	Muslim families are usually dysfunctional	——	——
29	Muslims most likely to end up receiving welfare assistance	——	——

Answers

Part I:

No. Question	Correct Answer	No. Question	Correct Answer
1	b	24	b
2	c	25	e
3	c	26	e
4	b	27	e
5	a	28	b
6	c	29	c
7	b	30	a
8	e	31	e
9	d	32	e
10	a	33	e
11	d	34	a
12	c	35	a
13	c	36	e
14	b	37	a
15	c	38	d
16	c	39	c
17	a	40	a
18	b	41	c
19	c	42	a
20	c	43	d
21	b	44	d
22	a	45	c
23	c		

Part II: *All answers must be "false." Any "true" answer suggests a lack of understanding and negative attitudes toward the Islamic religion and the Muslim people on the part of the reader. This makes reading this book of great value, particularly for students and professionals of the mental health fields.*

CHAPTER 1

Introduction

AMERICAN MUSLIMS IN COUNSELING

Islam is the fastest-growing religion in the world and in the United States. By the year 2010, Muslims in the United States will be the second-largest religious group after Christians (Bagby, 1994; Haddad & Lummis, 1987; Melton, 1993; Waugh, Abu Laban, & Qureishi, 1991). The rapid growth of the Muslim community is attributed mainly to immigration, a high fertility rate, and conversion. Despite this tremendous growth, the Muslim community continues to be understudied, widely misunderstood, and falsely stereotyped. Research and studies pertaining to the Muslim population with respect to counseling and other mental health fields is at best minimal and in most cases superficial and judgmental. Most of the few studies made on Muslims in mental health issues are based mainly on religious textual information that describe religious ideals and cultural norms rather than considering empirical data that indicate individual differences and social factors. Furthermore, these studies do not present counselors with practical requirements to understand, let alone accommodate their Muslim clients.

RACISM OR MULTICULTURALISM?

While trends of multiculturalism and inclusion are growing, Muslims continue to suffer rising racism. If racism is defined as the denial of access or opportunities, Muslims, particularly after the terrorist attacks of September 11, 2001, top the list of communities and populations that suffer from racism and prejudice according to FBI and the Council on American Islamic Relations reports.

The counseling profession is a helping one, and the counselor–client relationship is often defined as a helping and therapeutic one. To minority populations, it has not been always helpful. In fact, minority clients have constantly been victimized by racism despite the many efforts made to study and include much of the minority populations, (Poston, Craine, & Atkinson, 1991; Ridley, 1995). Muslims' victimization in counseling far exceeds that of other populations.

The wide spectrum of cultures in the United States has made American society unique and unparalleled in the world. Through immigration, political asylum, and the recruitment of exceptional scholars, the United States has opened its doors to a multitude of nationalities to the extent that it has become a microcosm of humanity. No other country has a greater variety of races, nationalities, and ethnic groups.

The report of the New York State Education Department (1991) observes that although the United States has provided asylum for diverse people, it has not allowed diverse cultures to survive. If not completely dissolved and assimilated, most of these cultures have been and often are, at best, marginalized.

It is encouraging, however, to note that within this diversity there is a growing awareness of pluralism. This pluralism represents a challenge to both majority and minority group members, although the tasks are different. For majority group members, the task is to feel the necessity of understanding and appreciating or at least respecting the values, mode of thinking, and behaviors of minority groups instead of perceiving them as inferior beings. For minority group members, the task is far more complicated. In addition to dealing with patterns of racism, they struggle to strike a balance between maintaining cultural integrity and experiencing forces of oppression and assimilation. This is not to say that assimilation is always and to any level undesirable. Rather, I refer to the forced assimilation that invalidates the right of minority groups to claim their heritage and values when they pose no threat to any legal code or violation to human rights.

Because of the growing trends of individualism, cultural differences are not limited to members of diverse populations only. They may include people of the same racial, ethnic, or religious populations. Pedersen (1988) defines multicultural counseling as "a situation in which two or more persons with different ways of perceiving their social environment are brought together in a helping relationship" (p. viii). Such expansion of the definition of multiculturalism is extremely useful in dealing with the Muslim population because of the wide diversity within its members.

Although many authors and researchers in the field use terms such as "multicultural" and "cross-cultural" interchangeably, some argue for the preference of the first to the latter. According to Pedersen (1988),

The term multicultural tends to be preferred over cross-cultural, intercultural, or transcultural because it describes a variety of co-equal cultures without comparing one culture to the other. By implying comparison, the terms cross-cultural, intercultural, and transcultural sometimes implicitly suggest that one culture is better than the other. (p. viii)

THE CHALLENGE AND THE OPPORTUNITY

The American Muslim community is so diverse that it represents all geographical regions of the globe and includes people of all racial and ethnic backgrounds. Therefore, while members of the Muslim community on the one hand share one religion and a set of values that differentiate them from members of other religious groups, on the other hand the Muslim community is diverse and consists of many subcultures and subgroups. Diversity among Muslims can be attributed to many variables, such as cultural, ethnic, regional and age-, language-, and class-related ones or even to differences related to the variation in understanding of and the level of commitment to Islam itself.

This diversity presents the counseling profession with both an opportunity and a problem. The opportunity is the inclusion of Muslims in counseling by discovering effective counseling methods, strategies, and techniques that are appropriate for helping Muslims deal with their concerns. Such inclusion will constitute a remarkable achievement for counselors and the counseling profession. The problem, however, is how to accurately understand this widely diverse group despite the many variables that determine the needs and shape the attitudes of its members. While Islam is a factor in the types of needs and problems that Muslim clients experience, clearly it is not the only one. Self-evident negative anti-Muslim publicity, stereotypes, discriminatory practices, and unfriendly attitudes toward Islam and Muslims in the United States further exacerbate the problem.

To properly include Muslims in counseling, we must reexamine the sources of our information on Islam and our attitudes toward Muslims. Furthermore, we must understand how Islam interacts with other individual and collective variables, such as race, culture, age, class, and education, thus producing a multitude of values and practices that are woven into daily life in complex, invisible ways.

THE PROFESSIONAL DUTY OF COUNSELORS

The effectiveness of counselors depends mainly on their ability to meet their professional obligations. By providing counselors with accurate, genuine, and true representations of American Muslims through the experiences of Muslim clients themselves, this book serves as the first, yet most important one in aiding counselors to meet their professional obligations. In this book, Muslim clients describe their experiences in counseling, particularly their perception of counseling, the barriers to seeking counseling, the issues for which they would and would not seek counseling, and proper counseling settings, approaches, techniques, and strategies. This will enhance the ability of professionals to accommodate Muslim clients. Draguns (1989) states, "The consensus among modern counselors is to accommodate culturally different clients instead of rejecting them" (p. 5).

Furthermore, the professional obligation of counselors is not completed by the conclusion of the counseling session or intervention. Rather, it must include the struggle to change the social institutions that are biased against their clients. Counselors who do not at least ask the question about whether the best interests of the client are served by existing social institutions—and whether those institutions can be changed at least in small ways—are failing in their professional obligations (Pedersen, 1988).

THEORETICAL FRAMEWORK

Multicultural counseling is fairly new, a fact that is symptomatic of the problem of understanding and changing views and approaches to other cultures. In the early 1970s, there were no books on counseling and culture (Draguns, 1989). Although increased in volume, subsequent literature shows an inadequate discussion of multicultural issues (Draguns, 1989; Ridley, 1995). To make the problem even worse, some counselors ignore that they even have biases or prejudices. A number of studies (Jones & Seagull, 1977; Pomales, Claiborn, & LaFromboise, 1986; Poston et al., 1991) strongly recommend that counselors take racial differences into account rather than project a color-blind image. Clients view counselors' color-blindness as a sign of insecurity or arrogance in refusing to admit cultural differences (Poston et al., 1991).

Having said that, it is necessary to note that counselor biases have become the preoccupation of most multicultural studies without giving adequate space to minority populations, their needs, or their values. It is assumed that self-awareness will lead counselors to accept their biases and consequently treat people of other cultures equitably (Ridley, 1995).

This book, however, takes a new approach; it provides accurate representation of Muslims by allowing Muslim individuals to speak for themselves and describe their own experiences and concerns. Using the symbolic interaction approach and acknowledging the influence of religion and culture on each other to various degrees and levels, I only facilitate the process of understanding Muslims' interpretations of their counseling experiences.

According to Pedersen (1988),

The counselor has only two choices: to ignore the influence of culture or to attend to it. In either case, however, culture will continue to influence a client's behavior with or without the counselor's awareness. (p. vii)

Symbolic interaction allows the particular group members to develop their own meanings, perspectives, and values underlying their activities. The basic principle of symbolic interaction is that all objects, events, and situations acquire their meanings through the process of human interpretation. The meanings attached to objects, events, and situations are not built in to them. Bogdan and Biklen (1992) state,

Basic to the approach (i.e., Symbolic Interaction) is the assumption that human experience is mediated by interpretation. Objects, people, situations, and events do not possess their own meaning; rather, meaning is conferred on them. (p. 36)

People, therefore, get the opportunity to express the meanings they construct for themselves and to include them in their interpretation. At the same time, symbolic interaction encompasses all other factors that may have contributed to the development of such meanings and interpretations. Bogdan and Biklen (1992) state,

Interpretation is not an autonomous act, nor is it determined by any particular force, human or otherwise. Individuals interpret with the help of others, people from their past, writers, family, television personalities and persons they meet in settings in which they work or play—but others do not do it for them. (p. 36)

Understanding a group of people in a cultural context requires more than just reading about or observing that particular group. Abu-Lughod (1990) cited Geertz: "The anthropologist can not simply observe behavior but must try to figure out what peoples' actions mean, to themselves and to others" (p. 86). The counselor and the psychologist should be no different.

Bearing that in mind, I must state that most literature about Islam and Muslims in the West, general and/or psychological, is neither representative nor accurate. Negative preconceived notions about Islam and Muslims do not allow for an accurate understanding of this population.

To illustrate this fact, American Muslims are often projected as "foreign," as of "the Orient," or as "the other," including indigenous American Muslims, blacks, and whites, even though the United States is the only country they have ever been in. A white Muslim woman whose ancestors fought in the Revolutionary War reported to me that just because of her Islamic dress, a fellow shopper screamingly instructed her to go home to Saudi Arabia. This puts the Muslim population in a doubly vulnerable position. If Muslims can escape racism that is based on racial differences or complexities, they might not be able to escape discrimination that is based on religious differences that can be easily recognized, particularly in the case of women wearing Islamic dress. In another case, an accomplished female graduate student of journalism in a prestigious university, because of either wearing the head scarf, her Muslim name, or both was asked by another student's parent if she finds learning English as a second language difficult.

Understanding the Muslim community requires, among other things, good knowledge of what things mean to Muslims themselves. The way people dress or believe has never been indicative of their national origin. According to Becker and Geer (1958), "We often do not understand that we do not understand and are thus likely to make errors in interpreting what is said to us" (p. 29). They also state,

Any social group, to the extent that it is a distinctive unit, will have to some degree a culture differing from that of other groups, a somewhat different set of common understandings around which action is organized, and these differences will find expression in a language whose nuances are peculiar to that group and understood only by its members. Members of churches speak differently from members of informal tavern groups: more importantly, members of any particular church or tavern group have cultures, and languages in which they are expressed, which differ somewhat from those of other groups of the same general type. (p. 29)

Religion and Culture

The intersection of religion and culture is very interesting and, at the same time, problematic. According to Geertz (1968) and adopted by Taibi (1991), "Religion is a cultural system that forms models for reality which relate to the human perceptions of reality" (p. 8). "These models of reality are not, therefore, penetrable experimentally but only interpretatively" (Geertz, 1968, p. 170; Taibi, 1991, p. 2).

As Geertz (1968) argues, "Religious content has a dual aspect: It conveys for its adherents meanings to current social and psychological realties, thereby acquiring 'an objective conceptual form'; they are both shaped by reality and at the same time shape reality to themselves" (p. 93). I find Geertz's (1973) definition of religion to be most effective, particularly for our study. This definition approaches religion as

(1) a system of symbols which act to (2) establish powerful, pervasive, and long-lasting modes of motivations in men by (3) formulating conceptions of a general order of existence and (4) clothing these conceptions with such an aura of factuality that (5) the moods and motivations seem uniquely realistic. (p. 90)

The term "culture" is very difficult to define (Bogdan & Biklen, 1992) to the extent that some authors reported more than 150 definitions for it

(Pedersen, 1988). However, it is related, among other things, to group structures, characteristics, and social behavior (Bogdan & Biklen, 1992; Geertz, 1973; Spradley, 1980). To Crollius (1984), "Culture often refers to a group of people whose members have in common distinct historical, linguistic and, often religious traditions, while geographic and racial factors can play a role in the constitution of such a group" (p. 47). In order to guard against generalizations that have often victimized members of the Muslim population, I intentionally include the factors of individuality and subgroup formation within the larger group. To elaborate, within each culture, there are subgroups that are identified by additional factors, including age, gender, profession, economic status, political affiliation, and sectarian affiliation within the one religious group.

Individual characteristics, particularly in a predominantly individualistic society such as that of the United States, also play a major role in the formation of the individual's choices and behavior. The individual's worldview should be recognized as a holistic concept that ties together the belief systems, values, lifestyles, and modes of dealing with others. Through this worldview, the person perceives his or her relationship to the world, including other people, institutions, nature, or things (Ibrahim, 1991; Pedersen, Fukuyama, & Heath, 1989; Sue, 1978). Applying this theoretical approach to American Muslims will help us more accurately understand the issues related to Muslims in counseling.

While most Muslims are taught Islam as encompassing every aspect of life from birth to death, including the relationship of its adherents to other people and to society (Farah, 1994), it is not the only force that affects the lives of Muslims, nor is it immune from being affected by other cultural and societal forces. To explain, Islam, on the one hand, forms a belief system that contributes to the shaping of the general features of Muslims' identity, perception of self and others, processes of thinking, social behaviors, political preferences, and economic and financial practices, to name only a few. On the other hand, religious beliefs, practices, and perceptions of life, to a great extent, are influenced by the various cultures and traditions of Muslim societies, historic or contemporary. This is illustrated by the different approaches as well as responses in different cultures to the same religious teachings. Therefore, assuming that Islam is the lone influence in the lives of Muslims or that Islam itself is immune from being influenced by cultural and individual factors will only further the misunderstanding of Islam and Muslims. For this reason, while we must consider the extent to which the Islamic religion influences the formation of motives, feelings, and practices of many Muslims, we cannot ignore the effects that cultural and societal factors have on the lives of Muslims and on their perceptions of reality.

In addition to the wide range of diversity of Muslim cultures and groups, there is also the individual factor in interpreting, acting, accepting, or rejecting on the basis of, among other things, education, experience, likes and dislikes, and personal circumstances. These factors lead an individual to be distinct from others, even from his or her own family members.

In comparing Muslim communities around the world with those of the United States, there is no doubt that tendencies of individualism in the American cultures are stronger than they are in any other Muslim community or culture, particularly those existing in the non-Western world. Thus, individualism among American Muslims can exert a greater influence on religious beliefs and societal norms, as well as on cultural practices of Muslims, more than individualism does in any other Muslim community and culture. Such individual factors must also be considered when attempting to understand American Muslims' beliefs, values, and cultures, especially in relation to the mental health professions.

Therefore, American Muslims, because of religious, cultural, and individual variables, can be more accurately described as having many subgroups where each group is distinct because of the following factors:

(a) The group's combination of religious, racial, ethnic, geographical, historical, and linguistic characteristics

(b) The affiliation to a subgroup due to factors such as age, gender, profession, education, social and economic status, political affiliation, religious sectarianism, and so on

(c) The level of individualism, including the level of assimilation and Americanization that is acquired by the individual

Having said that, I must note that Western psychology and counseling are based on Western philosophies, human development theories, and empirical findings (Badri, 1979; Jafari, 1993). This approach to understanding human behavior is often criticized as "ethnocentric." It accepts only one way of understanding reality and measures all cultural expressions according to the standards of this culture. By imposing Western values and lifestyles on non-Western clients, this approach deprives Western counseling of the values and support systems other cultures can provide. This means that culturally unaware and insensitive counselors will be less likely to understand the motives and behaviors of their Muslim clients and their clients' resistance to any imposition of values, and that both the counselor and client will be deprived of the traditional values and support systems that are a part of Muslim culture.

The same can be said about assessment of normality and deviance, counseling approaches and techniques, and objectives of counseling.

INTRODUCING CLIENTS

The criteria for selecting clients to include in this book were that they were adult individuals who had undergone professional counseling before coming to me. Younger clients were included during the process of family counseling. I have purposefully selected individuals from diverse backgrounds in terms of gender, social class, financial status, ethnic background, and religious conviction. The criteria for categorizing the religious conviction of an individual are based only on how clients perceive themselves. In order to compensate for the lack of representation of a particular group, I use information from the literature whenever possible.

A brief introduction of the participants illustrates their diversity. The names used in this book are pseudonyms in order to protect the identity of clients. Wahida is a white American woman in her late thirties. She converted to Islam when she was young, married a Middle Eastern man, and lived in the Middle East for more than 10 years. Currently, she lives in the United States after having divorced her husband and marrying an American Muslim. Aslam is a computer engineer in his mid-twenties. While he is originally from India, he currently holds Canadian citizenship and works in the United States. Farida, an Arab immigrant woman suffering from issues related to her handicapped son, was further traumatized by the murder of her husband. Labibah is a U.S.-born female college student. Pride is a housewife who comes originally from the Indian subcontinent and has been in the United States for more than 25 years.

Hikmat is a Ph.D. graduate from a U.S. university and a senior researcher in the United States. His wife is a homemaker. Their daughter is a U.S.-born graduate student who brought the family to therapy because she was suffering from eating-disorder problems. The Abed family migrated from Palestine as a result of the Palestinian–Israeli conflict. The husband received his education in his home country and presently works as a business owner. The wife received no education at all and stays home. This family, who is extremely closed to involving outsiders in their private affairs (the norm in most Arab cultures), participated in this study as a result of a conflict with the middle school of their two teenage daughters. Their son, a high school student, reported discriminatory practices made against him by his teachers, classmates, and counselors.

The economic status of these participants included those who are under poverty-line income, middle class, as well as affluent. The issues for which these participants have gone to counseling vary to a great extent, as will be explained later.

In addition to client participants, I have interviewed three counselors, one formally and two informally. One of these counselors I came to meet through our membership in the Multicultural Committee of the Mental Health Association, which I chaired. During our work together, we developed a friendship and began cooperation on various professional tasks. I also referred several Muslim clients to him for services that were beyond my expertise or because of other limitations. The second counselor was a school therapist who came to my office seeking information on how to deal with Arab and Muslim students and families. Later, I became involved with the school, school district, students, and their family in the case that is recorded in this book. The third counselor also contacted me for information on religious issues that one of her Muslim clients was facing.

These counselors vary in age, sex, multicultural education, and professional expertise. More details are provided as it becomes necessary.

QUESTIONS FOR DISCUSSION

1. How does the author define "religion" and "culture"? Debate the author's view citing practical situations.
2. How do Islam and cultures of Islam affect each other?
3. Why is it important to include Muslims in counseling?
4. What are the factors needed to take into account when attempting to understand American Muslims?
5. How does the author understand the difference between "multiculturalism" and "cross-cultural"? What are your personal preferences in this regard?
6. The author argues that the professional duty of the counselor does not end at showing sensitivity to the client. According to the author, what are other aspects of counselor's professional duty? How do you view the counselor's duty toward clients in light of that of the author?
7. What are the opportunities and challenges the American Muslim community presents to the counseling profession? Mention examples from your own experience that relate to Muslims or to other minority communities.

CHAPTER 2

Islam: The Religion and the Cultures

ISLAM IN THE WORLD

Islam is the youngest of the major monotheistic world religions. It is also the second-largest and the fastest-growing religion in the world (Bernstein, 1993; Cooper, 1993; Esposito, 1993, 1999; Roudi, 1988). Islam is also one of the fastest-growing religions in the United States (Marquand & Andoni, 1996b). Haddad and Lummis (1987) described Islam as an "American phenomenon" and predicted that, by the twenty-first century, it will be the second-largest religious community in the United States. The number of Muslims in the world is approximately 1.2 billion, one-fifth of the world's population. They exist in over 100 countries on all continents. The largest percentage of the Muslim population in the world exists in Asian countries. According to 2000 estimates, Indonesia, for instance, has 198.7 million Muslims, Pakistan has 140.2 million, while Bangladesh has 115.5 million (*Encyclopaedia Britannica Almanac,* 2003; *The New York Times Almanac,* 2002). The Muslim minority in India is more than 140 million, which is much larger than the number of Muslims in all Arab countries combined (*Encyclopaedia Britannica Almanac,* 2003; *The New York Times Almanac,* 2002). Esposito (1999) states,

To speak of the world of Islam today is not to refer to countries that stretch from North Africa to Southeast Asia but also to Muslim minority communities that exist across the globe. Thus, for example, Islam is the second or third largest religion in Europe and the Americas. (p. ix)

Most people were unaware of the presence of Muslims in Europe until the terrifying images of ethnic cleansing of Bosnian Muslims in the midst of Europe were brought to every home by various media outlets. Haddad and Lummis (1987) declare,

Attention is being given to the presence of Muslims not only in China and the Soviet Union but also in places like Japan, Australia and South Africa. There are substantial minority communities in the heart of Europe in Germany, Belgium, France and Great Britain, and in both the South and North American continent. (p. 155)

Islam began in Mecca in Arabia with the Prophet Muhammad and spread to every corner in the world.

"Islam," from an Arabic root that means "peace," means submission to the will of Allah, the Arabic name of God that is used by both the Jews and the Christians of the Arab world. Religiously speaking, a Muslim is any adult male or female who consciously witnesses that "there is no god but the One God and Muhammad is the Prophet of God." Islam encompasses the relationships of the adherents to each other and to their society from birth until death. Simply put, to most Muslims Islam provides a total way of life (Altareb, 1996; Carter & El-Hindi, n.d.; Farah, 1994; Haneef, 1993; Mawdudi, 1980; Voll, 1991). Islam, which began in the seventh century, spread across the world and became the second largest of the world's religions. During the course of history, Islam was not simply a spiritual community; rather, it also became a state and an empire.

Islam developed into a religiopolitical movement in which religion was integral to state and society. Voll (1991) states, "Muslims have a guide to and model that covers the most mundane aspects of every day life and behavior as well as the general principles directing the community" (p. 206). Politics also is included in Islam. Esposito (1991) argues, "Muslims' belief that Islam embraces faith and politics is rooted in its divinely revealed book, the holy Qur'an, and the example (Sunnah) of its founder/prophet Muhammad, and thus has been reflected in Islamic doctrine, history and politics" (p. 3).

The Community of Muslims

The following table 2.1 and figures 2.1–2.8 indicate the countries with the largest Muslim population in the world. The population of individual countries of each continent is followed by the percentage of the Muslim population for these countries, respectively. Though Islam recognizes that individuals will hold various loyalties, one's ultimate loyalty is expected to be to the community of faith, or *ummah* (Al-Ahsan, 1992). Despite the fact that Muslims make up different ethnicities, races, nationalities, and backgrounds, the unity of faith binds them into one community (Al-Ahsan, 1992).

Table 2.1
Countries with Largest Muslim Populations

No	Country	Number of Muslims	Continent
1	Indonesia	185,034,040	Asia
2	Pakistan	138,976,937	Asia
3	India	123,186,924	Asia
4	Bangladesh	112,629,660	Asia
5	Turkey	64,374,588	Europe
6	Iran	60,650,552	Asia
7	Egypt	58,062,710	Africa
8	Nigeria	55,593,204	Africa
9	Algeria	55,593,204	Africa
10	Morocco	28,739,971	Africa
11	Afghanistan	26,303,553	Asia
12	Sudan	25,364,240	Africa
13	Iraq	22,398,720	Asia
14	Saudi Arabia	21,983,262	Asia

Islam mandates that its followers establish a strong community based on faith. In fact, the Qur'an requires a strong communal bond among the Muslims as a necessary step to realize God's purpose on earth (Denny, 1995). Through this strong brotherhood, Islam eradicates racism and distinction among people of different cultures or class systems. Al-Faruqi (1984) states, "By affirming the brotherhood of all peoples, Islam denies the concept of ethnocentrism and the doctrine of election. As a universal religion, it aspires to include all nations within the Islamic state" (p. 59). Although the *ummah* (one nation) concept is widely popular among Muslims, this concept is not, to some extent, foreign to other communities of faith, including Judaism and Christianity (Voll, 1991). The unique feature in Islam, however, is that while there are no fundamental doctrinal differences among the various geographically scattered communities of the Muslim *ummah,* they are widely diverse culturally.

Figure 2.1
Population in African Countries

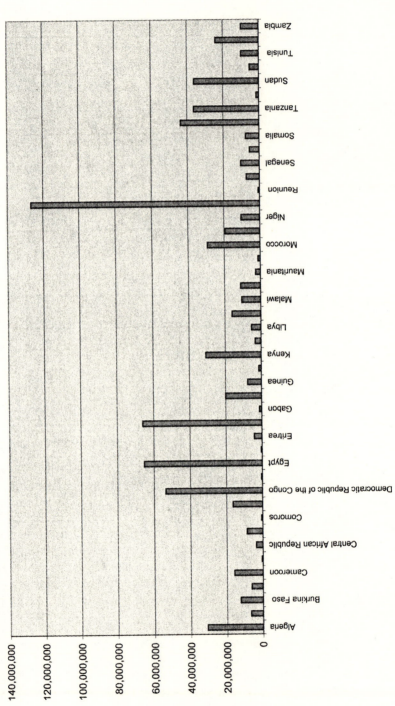

Figure 2.2
Percentage of Muslims in African Countries

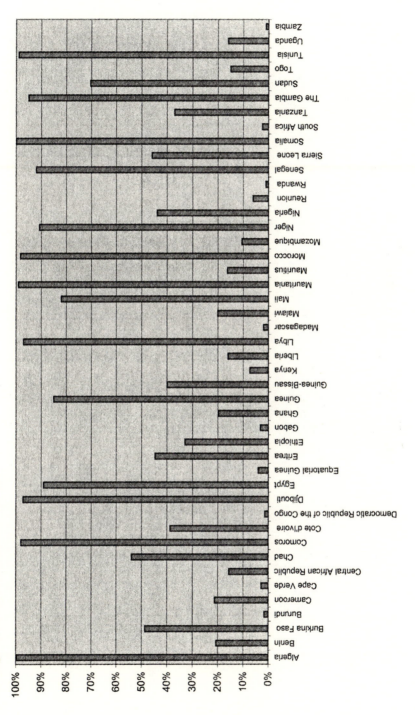

15

Figure 2.3
Population in Asian Countries

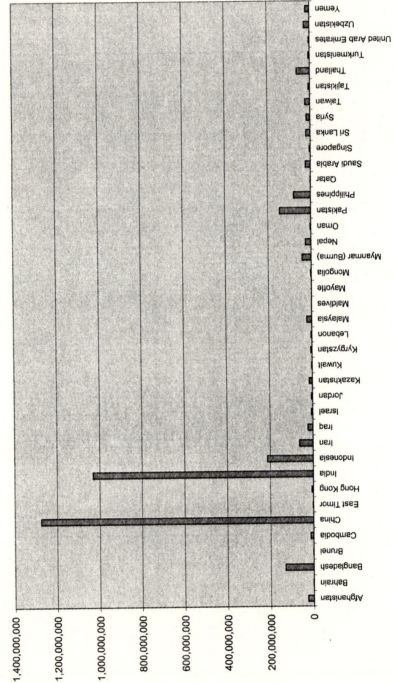

Figure 2.4
Percentage of Muslims in Asian Countries

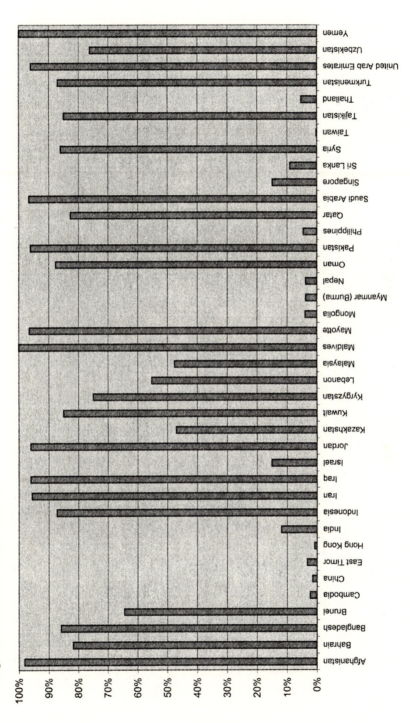

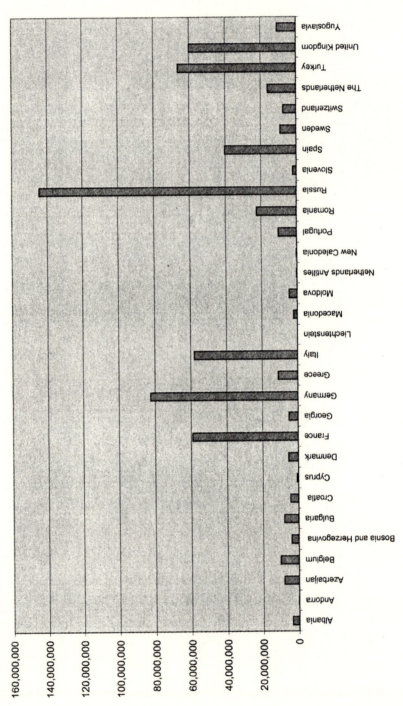

Figure 2.5
Population in European Countries

18

Figure 2.6
Percentage of Muslims in European Countries

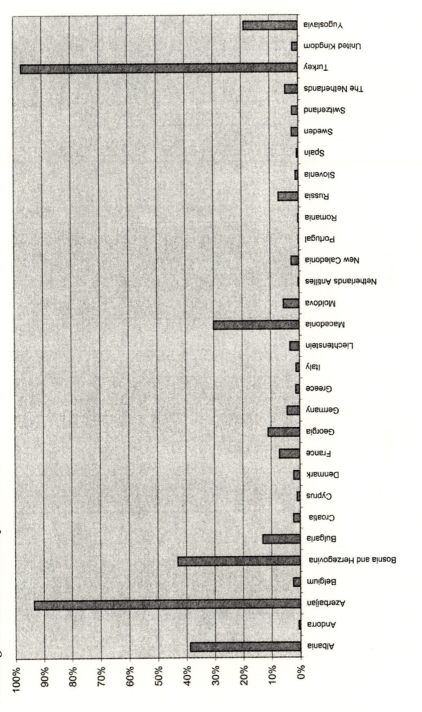

19

Figure 2.7
Population in South America

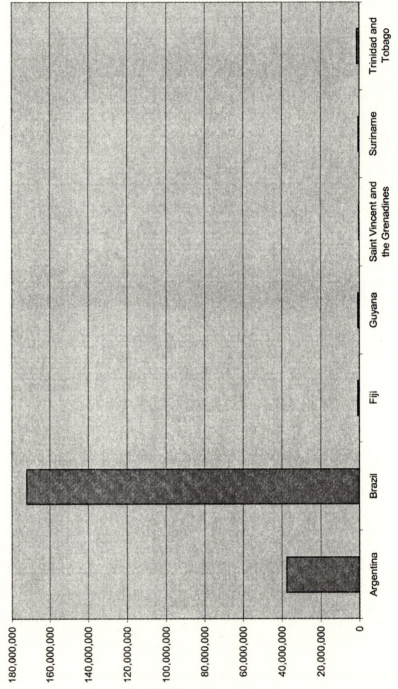

Figure 2.8
Percentage of Muslims in South America

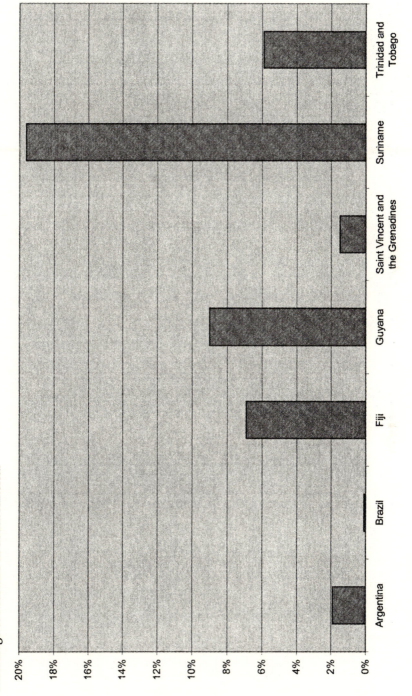

Muslims also value family and group affiliation, including friends and communities. Hedayat-Diba (2000) states, "Muslims are a highly group-minded and socially affiliative people. They value family and close friends above all else. They are generous, hospitable, and loyal to a fault. In America, the mosque has become central to an Islamic lifestyle" (p. 300).

To sum up, Muslims of the world are unified by the five Islamic tenets of faith and by their obligation to form an *ummah*.

Tenets of Islam

While faith in God, the Qur'an, and the Prophet Muhammad unite Muslims in their common belief, the five pillars of Islam provide a unity of practice in the midst of rich diversity. The five pillars are the common denominator, the five essential obligatory practices that all Muslims must follow (Esposito, 1995). They are (a) *shahadah* (the profession of faith), (b) *salat* (prayer), (c) *zakat* (almsgiving), (d) *sawm* (fasting), and (e) *hajj* (pilgrimage). To understand the significance as well as the influence of each of these tenets on the lives of Muslims, I provide the following more detailed information.

Shahadah *(Profession of Faith)*

For Muslims, a declaration of faith identifies the belief that there is no god but God and that Muhammad is the last Messenger (Al-Faruqi, 1984). By uttering this declaration, one becomes a follower of Islam (Farah, 1994). It also makes Muslims aware that only God has supreme power and that it is their duty to emulate the exemplary life of the Prophet Muhammad (Al-Faruqi, 1984; Altareb, 1996; Farah, 1994). *Shahada* is the first few spoken words a newborn baby hears and the last a dying person would speak (Farah, 1994). It, therefore, acts as a source of identity. It also helps bind Muslims in the community of faith (*ummah*) and at the same time helps overcome barriers of race, ethnicity, national origin, language, or culture (Altareb, 1996; Haddad & Lummis, 1987).

Salat *(Prayer)*

Salat is the second pillar of Islam and the supreme act of worship in Islam (Al-Faruqi, 1984). Many Muslims disagree with the translation of the Salat into prayer. Al-Faruqi (1984) states, "It is mistakenly referred to as "prayer." The latter is an act of adoration or worship possible in any shape, form, language or condition . . . *Per contra*, Salat may be performed only at certain times, in a prescribed way, under certain conditions" (p. 142).

Salat in the Arabic language means "connection." The sole purpose of *salat* in Islam is to connect Muslim worshipers with their Lord. There are five daily prescribed prayers: at dawn, at midday, in the afternoon, after sunset, and at night. These prayers are short and require bowing and prostration. It is common to see devout Muslims praying additional voluntary prayers. Muslims may pray anywhere provided that the place is clean and that there are no distractions, preferably in congregation, facing Mecca. They are required to worship as a community on Fridays at midday and on two major holidays. The Qur'an describes the benefit of prayer as "restrains from shameful and evil deeds" (Qur'an 29:45, trans. Ali, p. 1164). Altareb (1996) states, "If Muslims dutifully practice *Salat*, then they can not stray too far off God's path, for they will have to face God during dawn, midday, afternoon, after sunset, and night" (p. 32).

The performance of *salat*, therefore, allows Muslims to be mindful of the right behavior in the midst of worldly activities. It also provides the strength and support to individuals that help them deal with difficult situations and challenges of life.

Zakat *(Charity)*

The third pillar of Islam is also referred to as "almsgiving," "poor tax," or "poor-due" and literally means the purification of one's own self from greed and miserliness while purifying one's own wealth through giving to the poor. It also serves as an "expiation" or "purification" of what the Muslim retains of material possessions (Farah, 1994). By giving to the poor of one's own honest earnings, seeking no return or reciprocity, the Muslim is doing both an act of worship and an act of community. This pillar helps the rich show their compassion and, at the same time, rids the poor of ill feelings against those who are well off. According to Sachedina (1997), "In a number of poor Muslim countries this benevolence provided by wealthy individuals has underwritten badly needed social services for those who can not afford them" (p. 32).

The institution of *zakah* gives the person, giving or receiving, a sense of worth and value, thus connecting with and belonging to the community.

Sawm *(Fasting)*

Fasting means abstinence from food, drinks, and sensual pleasures, particularly sexual intercourse, from dawn until sunset during the month of Ramadan, which is the ninth month of the Islamic lunar calendar. In the month of Ramadan, the Prophet Muhammad received his first revelation of the Qur'an. Since the lunar calendar is some ten days shorter than the solar year, the fasting and all Muslim festivals occur in different seasons. Fasting is prescribed only for every healthy, adult Muslim. Exempted from fasting are children, the sick, and those for whom fasting may constitute physical or mental harm, such as travelers as well as hard laborers. Esposito (1995) writes, "The primary emphasis is not so much on self mortification as such but rather on spiritual self-discipline, reflection, and the performance of good works" (p. 246). The end of Ramadan is marked by a great festival, Eid Ul-Fitr, after which life returns to normal. Eid Ul-Fitr is one of the two greatest religious holidays in Islam. Family members, relatives, and friends join to feast and exchange gifts in a celebration that lasts in many cultures for three days (Esposito, 1995).

In addition to strengthening one's relationship with God, disciplining one's soul, and preparing the person for possible future hardships, fasting also makes the rich empathize with those who are less fortunate and feel for a month what they always go through. Fasting in community and celebrating the end of fast also in community along with all Muslims of the world help bring Muslims into a unity both religiously and socially.

Fasting makes people aware of their abilities and discipline, thus giving them a sense of confidence to make other changes in life as they become necessary.

Hajj *(Pilgrimage)*

The fifth religious duty of the Muslim is pilgrimage to the sacred monuments of Mecca at least once in a lifetime for those who are physically and financially able. Pilgrimage takes place during the first 13 days of the twelfth month of the Islamic calendar year. More than two million Muslims attend pilgrimage every year. They come from short distances as well as from the farthest places on earth, allowing participants to experience the universality of Islam. From the experience of those who have performed it, *hajj* is overwhelmingly moving: the pilgrims are changed for good (Altareb, 1996). Sachedina (1997) states, "The pilgrimage brings together Muslims of diverse cultures and nationalities to achieve a purity of existence and a communion with God that will exalt the pilgrims for the rest of their lives" (p. 33).

Muslims who are not present at Mecca at the time of pilgrimage still celebrate its events at home with their own community.

The Islamic Worldview

To Al-Faruqi and Al-Faruqi (1986), "The Islamic world-view is based mainly on *Tawhid* (the Unity of God) as a general view of reality, of truth, of the world, of space and time, of human history" (p. 74). Rashid (1990) suggests that the Islamic worldview consists of "(a) Innate goodness of human beings, (b) Moral absolutism, (c) Unitary concept of Creator, (d) Brotherhood based on faith, (e) Women as mothers of civilization, (f) Domination of the earth is for Allah (God), and (g) Unity of knowledge" (p. 19).

An individual is, therefore, expected to carry out God's will instead of his or her own because of the realization that Allah is the origin of every-thing and that Allah is the final goal (Al-Faruqi, 1984). Failing to adhere to the mandates of Islam does not necessarily mean that the individual is happy with such lack of adherence. Jamilah, one of my clients, states,

I feel guilty that I don't wear the veil. I feel guilty that God took my husband and gave me this [disabled] son because I don't obey him in everything I do. I feel guilty if, by any chance, I—like—swear at my kids, or (my husband) if I said something like this, I feel guilty. I talk to the therapist about it. Every step of the way, I feel sometimes I'm 100 percent Muslim because Islam is a big part of my life.

"Islam" and "Muslims"

It is important to note that the notion of "Islam is a way of life" refers to the comprehensive and inclusive nature of the Islamic ideals. Islam as a religion must not to be equated or confused with the practices of Muslim individuals. In most cases, the legacy of thought, action, and expression by Muslims is understood as constitutive of Islam itself. Therefore, the following two assumptions have dominated media, academia, and other circles when writing and reporting on Islam and Muslims: First, the reli-gion of Islam and the cultures of Muslims are often viewed as one and the same when in fact they are not, and, second, Muslims are often and erroneously reduced to a group of identical people, thus linking the crimes of individual Muslims to the religion of Islam. Such portrayals have caused a great deal of frustration among Muslims as terms like "Islamic terrorism," "Islamic extremism," and "Islamic violence" are tirelessly re-peated. The consequences of these portrayals manifest in the form of dis-crimination, prejudice, violence, and hate crimes against Muslims. Nine months after the September 11, 2001, tragedy, the Scripps Howard News Service (May 26, 2002) reported, "Hate crimes against Muslims, Arabs and Sikhs may have subsided, but allegations of workplace bias against them have mushroomed. The U.S. Equal Employment Opportunity Commis-sion says it filed 497 such bias claims since the terrorist attacks, compared to 193 during the comparable period the year before."

To explain further, the Islamic ideals, on the one hand, are often referred to as "Scriptural Islam." Woodward (1995) states, "Scriptural Islam is more than a religion. It is a detailed guide to human conduct, providing precise instruction in areas including personal hygiene, diet, dress, mar-riage, divorce, inheritance, taxation, and others. Particularly in the case of family law, the demands of the text often clash with long established cul-tural patterns" (p. 337).

On the other hand, Islam is defined according to Al-Faruqi (1984) as "the ideal to which all Muslims strive and by which they would and should be defined. Hence, true objectivity demands that Islam be distinguished from Muslim history and instead be regarded as its essence, its criterion and its measure" (p. xiii).

We must, therefore, differentiate between Islam as a religion and the various cultures of Muslims. Esposito (1995) states,

Islam as a religion refers to regulations pertaining to piety, ethics, beliefs and practices of worship. These spiritual aspects of worship are called "ibadat" and hence called "roots" or foundations of the faith, for instance, Allah's uniqueness, the final prophecy of prophet Muhammad, prayer, alms giving, fasting, and the pilgrimage to Mecca. On the other hand, Islam as a culture refers to the ideas and practices of Muslims in the context of changing social, economic, and political circumstances. People not only worship God, but also interact in social relationships called "mua'malat." (p. 323)

Islamic Calendar and Holidays

The Islamic calendar starts from the date of and commemorates the emigration of the Prophet Muhammad and his companions from Mecca, fleeing persecution and escaping attempts on his life to Medina, both in today's Saudi Arabia. This event is known as *Hijrah* and commonly referred to as *Hegira*. For Muslims, this event is the most significant in Islamic history, more than the birth and death of the Prophet himself because it "heralded the dawn of new era, the Islamic era, and the end of the 'Age of Ignorance' (*jahiliyah*)" (Farah, 1994, p. 47).

Muslim holidays follow the Islamic calendar, which is a lunar calendar in which the beginning of each month is signaled by the appearance of the new moon. Although it has 12 months, it is shorter than the Gregorian calendar because the number of days in each month ranges from 29 to 30 days only. The Islamic calendar year is approximately 11 days shorter than the Gregorian one, thus causing Islamic holidays to rotate throughout the year. Muslims follow no procedures to adjust the Hijri calendar to match the Gregorian one. Therefore, Muslims' holidays oftentimes fall on weekdays in which schools, colleges, and the private and public sectors are working and functioning. This puts American Muslims in the difficult position of trying to reconcile their study or work with their religious obligations. Muslim students would have to endure extraordinary difficulty while trying to attend their religious holidays and take an exam at the same time. Teachers and professionals are encouraged to accommodate the needs of their Muslim students and clients in this regard by discussing with their Muslim population if a hardship is being imposed and ways Muslim students can be allowed to attend their religious holidays without the risk of missing important discussions or exams. In the case of employees, I am confident that they would be eager to make up for the missed time by working extra hours or during holidays that are not their religious duties to attend. The following table (Table 2.2) shows the Muslim festivals and religious holidays in the Islamic lunar calendar. Due to the rotation of the holidays, educators, professionals, and employers should not show skeptical attitudes when a Muslim person presents the same religious holiday this year in a Gregorian date different than the previous year. To find out the corresponding dates in the Gregorian calendar, the reader is asked to consult any of the many organizers found in software format or printed texts, or even in Islamic Web sites. The holidays marked in table 2.2 represent those acknowledged by the wide range of Muslims around the world, although some groups may not recognize all of them.

Jihad and Terrorism

Jihad is one of the most misunderstood terms by both Muslims and non-Muslims alike. In the minds of many, jihad is translated as "a holy war to kill all infidels and impose the faith of Islam on others." The good news is that there is no place in Islam for a holy war and war was never considered or labeled as holy. War is conducted only in the case of necessity and under very strict rules. The Prophet's reported advice to his armies included the prohibition of cutting trees and killing animals, women, children, or elders. Furthermore, it stipulated not to disturb worshippers of other religions and to leave them to continue their devotion and worship. The term "infidels" is not an Islamic one either. People who are not Muslims are referred to in the Qur'an as either people of the book (i.e., Jews and Christians), unbelievers for those who reject faith in God and His Prophets, and *Mushrikoon* (i.e., polytheists) for those who worship other than the One God. Moreover, the imposition of Islam by force is prohibited by the Qur'anic stipulation in 2:256, which translates to: "Let be no compulsion in religion," simply because faith depends on conviction and free will, which is incompatible with faith. Scholars on the history of Islam such as Smith (1999) went even farther to state that "conversion to Islam was accepted, of course, but not encouraged" (p. 312).

The reader may ask then what does jihad mean according to Islam, and how does Islam view terrorism?

Jihad is derived from the Arabic root (j-h-d) that means efforts and struggle. The word jihad means "to strive and to struggle." The highest form of jihad, according to Islam, is an individual's strife to rid his or her soul of its evil tendencies. Arrogance and prejudice rank highly on the list of such evils. Jihad includes various forms of peaceful encounters such as those of words, the pen, and financially—and finally by weapons. The Qur'an instructs the Prophet to argue against his opponents by the means that are best (e.g., "And dispute ye not with the People of the Book [i.e., Christians and Jews], except with the means that are best" [Qur'an 29:46]),

Table 2.2
Islamic Calendar and Holidays

No.	Month	Date	Name of the holiday	Significance
1	Muharram	1st	Islamic new year	2004 A.D. corresponds to 1424/1425 A. H.
		9th and 10th	Tasu'ah and Ashura (i.e. 9th and 10th)	Sunnis celebrate this occasion, known in Judaism as the Passover, while Shiites celebrate only the 10th for the martyrdom of Imam Husain.
2	Safar	N/A		
3	Rabe'i Awwal (i.e. First Rab'i)	12th	Mawlid an-Nabi (birthday of the Prophet)	While the birth of the Prophet is revered by all Muslims, some Muslims may consider its celebration an unacceptable addition to the religion of Islam since it is not mentioned in the Qur'an or expressed by the Prophet. This also explains the apprehension of many Muslims in regards to birthday occasions and celebrations.
4	Rabe'I Thani or Akhir (i.e. seond or Last Rabe'i)	N/A		
5	Jumada Awwal (i.e. First Jumada)	N/A		
6	Jumada Thani or Akhir (i.e. Second or Last Jumada)	N/A		
7	Rajab	27th	Isr'a and M'iraj	The night journey of the Prophet from Mecca to Jerusalem where he ascended to heavens. Not all Muslims celebrate it. During this journey, the five daily prayers were prescribed for Muslims.
8	Sha'aban	14th	The night of the 15th (middle) of Sha'aban.	Many Muslims spend the night in prayers, meditation and devotion.

Table 2.2
Continued

9	Ramadan	The whole month and especially the last 10 days and nights	Ramadan, last ten days and the night of Qadr (power) for the the night of 27th of Ramadan or of the last odd nights in the last 10 days.	Adult and healthy Muslims abstain from foods, drinks and sensual pleasure from dawn until sunset daily. During the nights, Muslims observe special extra prayers at the mosque called Taraweeh. For the specified nights, devout Muslims make extra efforts for worship and devotion.
10	Shawwal	1st – 3rd	Eidul-Fitr (Festival of breaking the fast)	Muslims pray in congregations in the early morning hours, attend a sermon, exchange gifts, visit each other and attend special festivities in the mosques, Islamic and cultural centers.
11	Dhul Q'idah	N/A		
12	Dhul Hijjah	8th–13th	Pilgrimage, the 9th is the Day of 'Arafah & the 10th is the day of Eidul Adha (Festival of Sacrifice)	Pilgrimage commemorates the rituals of Prophets Abraham, his son Ishmael and Muhammad. Muslims who are not performing Hajj would fast on the Day of 'Arafah. EidUl Adha is the culmination of Hajj rites and is celebrated by the sacrifice of an animal thus commemorating the attempt of the Prophet Abraham to sacrifice his son Ishmael who was ransomed with a ram by God.

by the means of the Qur'an (i.e., by using the argument and evidence of the Qur'an, which states, "Therefore, listen not to the unbelievers, but strive against them with the utmost strenuousness, with the Qur'an" [Qur'an 25:52]), and even when concluding an argument not to offend your opponents by telling them they are wrong (e.g., "and certain it is that either we or you are on right guidance or in manifest error!" [Qur'an 34/24]). Jihad in the form of fighting and war was not permitted in Islam until later, when, after 13 years of continued persecution and injustice against Muslims, they fled their homes, families, and properties to Medina. The Qur'anic stipulation that gave the permission to fight clearly stated the reasons for such fighting as to allow Muslims the right to defend themselves, stating the following: "To those against whom war is made, permission is given [to fight], because they are wronged; and verily, Allah is most powerful for their aid" (Qur'an 22:39). To assert that war can only be allowed when there is no other choice, the Qur'an instructs meeting evil with good, as it states, "Nor can goodness and evil be equal. Repel [evil] with what is better: then will he between whom and thee was hatred become as it were thy friend and intimate" (Qur'an 41:34). Since jihad is a religious term, it requires a religious definition and guidelines. The legal definition of the warring aspect of jihad is that it must be initiated by the Imam or caliph (i.e., a state legitimate authority) that is guided by the principles of justice as outlined by Islam. Violence, terrorism, and other acts of disruption to society in the name of jihad could be labeled as murder, robbery, rebellion, and so on—but not jihad. Individuals or groups that are waging wars against their own states' authorities, innocent human beings, and, in fact, the world are called in Islam *Bughat*, which means "aggressors," or *Muharibin*, which means "warring factions"—crimes for which there are severe penalties in the Islamic law.

Terrorism is an awful invention that violates many Islamic values and principles and carries a severe punishment in Islam. According to Islam, it is a violation of sanctity of life, property, and trust between members of the society. Islam clearly forbids suicide, murder, destruction of property, and betraying one's neighbors and fellow citizens. The worldwide Muslims are victimized by terrorism as much as, if not more than, anyone else. In addition to the damage to the name and reputation of Islam, terrorists do not distinguish Muslims from others when committing terrorist acts. Terrorism, however, is not the problem of the Muslim or Middle Eastern worlds alone. Rather, it is the world's phenomenon and problem. Therefore it must be dealt with as such in order to secure victory over terrorism and terrorists. The vast majority of ordinary and law-abiding Muslims must not be victimized because a few Muslims or Middle Easterners have gone mad. Many of the problems that Muslims have faced after each terrorist act—from the one that destroyed the Oklahoma Federal Building in 1995 to the September 11, 2001, attacks—include name-based, racial, and religious profiling, stigma, hate crimes, and blunt discrimination. Counselors and other professionals need to be aware of the social and political practices and trends in order to help their clients deal with such issues.

Implications for Counseling

Islam is a major force in the lives of most Muslims. It informs the thinking and behavior in social, economic, and professional aspects of life. Counselors can be helpful if they examine the religiosity of their Muslim clients and design help strategies, approaches, and goals accordingly. Various Islamic beliefs and practices can be used to strengthen the client's self-esteem and courage for the desired change.

The Islamic religion teaches responsibility and accountability, which provide individuals with the desire and ability to change. Counselors can greatly benefit their clients by utilizing this internal motivating force as well as by making clients partners in setting the goals of counseling.

Since Islam is not the only influence in the lives of Muslims, counselors must examine other factors and consider the client's immediate as well as long-term needs and concerns. Understanding the client's cultural background, level of religiosity, individual characteristics, and the specific circumstances represents the first step toward appropriate intervention.

If the client's issues are religion based, counselors can alienate and create distrust in their clients by attempting to minimize the importance of religion in the lives of their clients. Since Muslims believe in the responsibility and capability of individuals to uphold the highest ideals, behavioral therapy would prove most effective with Muslim clients.

As stated earlier, Islam presents itself as a total way of life. In Islamic cultures, the soul, mind, and body are interconnected and, therefore, influence one another in health as well as in illness. Illness, mental or physical, is seen as a lack of harmony between the inner and the outer self (Hedayat-Diba, 1999). Muslims may, therefore, react to illness differently. While some rely on God for a cure, others may consider seeking treatment as a religious obligation. For the first group, symptoms of mental dysfunctions may be neglected or denied for a long time, thus resulting in worsening the condition of the client. For the latter one, unquestioned authority will be given to the professional as the expert, thus resulting in passive attitudes that limit the client's participation in the setting of goals as well as in the development of treatment plans (Hedayat-Diba, 1999).

For Muslims who come from collectivistic societies, extended family structure and strong community support can prove very helpful to Muslim clients if adequately utilized by counselors. Nuclear Muslim families in the United States exist mainly because of economic pressures and/or reasons related to immigration policies. Islam in general advocates for the elderly. The adult children are expected to take care of their aging parents. There are no nursing homes in Muslim countries (Hedayat-Diba, 1999). In a study by Haddad and Lummis (1987), American Muslims were asked, "If it is too difficult or expensive to care for elderly parents at home, should a good care facility be found?" (p. 88). Almost half the respondents disagreed, yet slightly less than a fourth agreed, and slightly more than a fourth had mixed feelings. Hedayat-Diba (1999) states, "Muslims feel that going outside the extended family or immediate community to have their needs met is shameful, and much care is taken to avoid such embarrass-ment" (p. 299).

Counselors can help Muslim clients find a balance between remaining loyal to family and community while at the same time pursuing personal goals. Practical examinations of the client's options and the likely outcome can help reach solutions that are in the best interest of all, including the elders.

Internationally speaking, concerns of Muslim clients may be universal rather than limited to only domestic ones. Clients are likely to link inter-national events to domestic issues. To illustrate, a simple case of job dis-crimination, for instance, may be seen by the client as a part of a conspiracy that is linked to the historic conflicts between Europe and the Muslim world as well as to the present role of the United States in the Middle East conflict. Moreover, a Muslim client may be traumatized over news of civil war, natural disaster, famine, or other distressing news in some other parts of the Muslim world. Such trauma may be intensified if the client is di-rectly linked to the regions affected.

Counselors must, therefore, be well informed of issues related to their Muslim clients, historic and contemporary as well as international and domestic, and how they would impact the lives of their clients currently and in the future. Clients should also be encouraged to speak out and vent their concerns even when they do not appear to counselors that they have direct impact on the issues at hand. The variations and the urgency of issues affecting Muslim clients warrant that counselors be adequately pre-pared to select from among the available approaches and strategies the ones that best serve the particular clients at hand instead of indiscrimi-nately adhering to the approach of their preference. An example is the case of clients suffering trauma as a result of displacement (e.g., refugees) or job discrimination where financial needs and psychological stress require immediate intervention that cannot be served by the psychoanalytical ap-proach and techniques. Familiarity and competency in all different ap-proaches of human development and counseling theories in addition to the understanding of world issues are, therefore, necessary requirements for the effective counseling of Muslims.

With respect to Islamic religious practices, they are considered bona fide religious practices that are protected by the U.S. Constitution and federal and state laws. Knowledge of these Islamic principles and values should provide educators, administrators, and counselors with information on the basic needs for Muslims in educational institutions as well as the workplace. For instance, Muslim clients would need accommodations to perform their five daily prayers, to break their fast at sundown during the month of Ramadan, and to celebrate their religious holidays. They would also need time on Fridays to join the Islamic weekly congregation. Counselors can help clients with respect to these needs by demanding accommodations for Muslims to fulfill their religious obligations. With regard to fasting, for instance, employers and administrators should be made aware of the fact that, because of fasting, Muslim students and employees may not perform at their best at the end of the day during the month of Ramadan. Furthermore, they would need time to pray and break their fasting at the time of sunset. This may require alternative arrangements for employees to do their work and for students to take their exams at other times. In an unprecedented move aimed at promoting sensitivity and accommodating Muslim students, officials at Syracuse University issued a letter in the fall of 2000 urging faculty and administrators at the university to allow Muslim students time to break their fasting and pray at the time of sunset. Furthermore, they urged the university community to demonstrate sensitivity to Muslims by holding end-of-semester and holiday festivities, celebrations, or parties only after sundown in order to allow Muslim students the opportunity to participate whenever possible. If unable to make such arrangements, the university community was asked not to display food in the same room where Muslim students might be present while fasting. School counselors can help protect young Muslim students in schools who are fasting from being teased or made fun of by peers and classmates. During lunchtime, it would be insensitive to send fasting Muslim students to the cafeteria with all other students to sit idle while all others are eating and drinking. Instead, they can attend free time or structured programming at the library or in a room under supervision.

For academic and career counseling, studies and jobs related to the production, distribution, or promotion of materials that are forbidden Islamically, such as alcoholic beverages and gambling, may not be considered options by Muslim clients.

Counselors should, therefore, assist their Muslim clients in finding academic and career opportunities that do not conflict with their religious values.

Islamic Stages of Development

According to Islam, the developmental stages can be divided into (a) *mahd*, (b) *tufulah*, (c) *murahaqah*, (d) *shabab*, and (e) *kuhulah*. In the following section, I provide a brief overview of the main characteristics of these stages and their social implications.

Mahd *(Infancy)*

Every child is born, according to Islam, equipped with the pure internal instincts or nature called *fitra*. This stage can be subdivided into two sub-stages; *al-Mahd* (the cradle) and *radaa'* (breast feeding). In the first stage, parents are required to carry out some religious rituals, the lack of which are believed to affect the child's righteousness and functionality in the future. It becomes the child's responsibility to fulfill whatever parents failed to perform on his or her behalf in childhood. These rituals include calling the prayer in the right ear of the child immediately after birth; shaving his or her hair after one week; giving the hair's weight in gold or silver in charity; sacrificing a sheep or two to feed family, friends, and the poor in charity; and selecting a good name for the child on the same occasion (Kobeisy, 1997). While many Muslims take these rituals seriously and literally, others may not follow all the steps or the same order. During this stage of infancy, parents must provide good nurturing as well as lawfully earned nourishment. The Qur'an (2:233) puts special emphasis on a mother's breast feeding and gives two years as a minimum time period for it.

Tufulah *(Childhood)*

This stage lasts from the age of two until the age of puberty. It can, however, be subdivided into three substages: (a) childhood, (b) distinction, and (c) discipline.

Tufulah *(Childhood)*. In this stage (two to six), the child is characterized by curiosity and ability to imitate (Kobeisy, 1997). At this age, children are still being influenced the most by parents, by their family environment, and by that which is allowed and encouraged by their family, such as schools, friends, television, and so on (Kobeisy, 1997). Ali ibn Abi Taib, the third caliph of Islam and the Prophet's cousin and son-in-law, is reported to have said, "The heart of a child is like a receptive soil, everything sown in it will be accepted" (cited in At-Tall, 1990, p. 343).

Psychologically, children from the age of two to seven years are characterized by the desire to imitate adults in speech, gesture, and action. Thomas (1990) states, "The home environment exerts a particularly strong effect on the child's personal-social relations because it is from family members that the young derive their first taste of what the social world is like" (p. 110). These years are, therefore, crucial in the development of the child's personality (Kobeisy, 1997).

Tamieez *(Distinction)*. In this age (seven to nine), children are intentionally taught and trained. They are taught Islamic obligations, beliefs, and practices. Cultural practices and social norms are often confused with religious ones and are, therefore, introduced to children as religious. Furthermore, they are ready and eager to achieve and grow, or else their growth will be inhibited or delayed (Kobeisy, 1997). Erikson (1959) contends that "the child may have potential abilities which, if not evoked and nurtured during these years, may develop later or never" (cited in Thomas, 1990, p. 144). The age of seven marks the beginning of the distinction stage. This is based on a statement by the Prophet Muhammad instructing Muslims to teach their children prayers when they reach the age of seven. Other religious obligations, practices, societal norms, and traditions are also required at this age to allow for gradual training toward complete maturity at the age of puberty. Qur'anic injunctions also impose certain instructions on children of this age, such as requiring them to seek permission before entering the privacy of their parents at times of rest during the day and night (Qur'an 24:58). Traditional male/female roles and relationships are also introduced at this stage.

Ta'dib *(Discipline)*. In this stage, which starts at 10 and continues until the age of puberty, children are held accountable for not performing their religious duties.

This substage and the previous one are so delicately intersecting that many Muslim writers confuse them and call it "discipline" (see, e.g., At-Tall, 1990; Zahran, 1977).

Murahaqah *(Adolescence or Puberty)*

In this age, which starts as soon as the physical signs of puberty are experienced, adolescents are encouraged to take responsibility and make decisions. The term *murahaqah* suggests the presence of internal and external struggle. The internal one refers to the struggle between feelings and emotions on the one hand and the social norms and traditions on the other. Many of the adolescent's feelings and emotions cannot be freely expressed in most collectivist cultures. The external struggle refers to the view of one's self versus others' views of the person. While the adolescent wants to be treated like an adult, parents and elders still view him or her as a minor. Variations between cultural practices in the level of independence given to adolescents compared to expectations of them to adhere to adults' instructions can lead to very challenging times in dealing with this age-group. Islam pays special attention to the importance of monitoring friends and activities but not in a controlling manner. Some Islamic scholars report religious textual statements instructing to "allow your children to play for seven years, discipline for another seven years, and befriend for seven years more, then let them take responsibility of themselves." The instruction to befriend does not mean in any way to control.

After reaching this age, the adolescent is physically mature to practice adult life, including marriage. Contrary to American culture, which stipulates the age of 16 for driving, 18 for marriage, and 21 for drinking, the age of puberty is indicative of responsibility in Islamic religion and most Islamic cultures. Many Muslims criticize American culture for treating adolescents like children, thus delaying their ability to take responsibility for their own actions.

Shabab *(Youths)*

This stage starts after 20 years of age and continues until the age of 40 to 45. It is characterized by more maturity, stability, and rationalization (Attar, 1987).

Kuhulah *(Adults)*

This stage starts from age 40 and continue until old age. It represents the peak of one's maturity physically, emotionally, and intellectually. It also marks the beginning of decline, particularly physically and intellectually.

Each stage of development is characterized by a set of attitudes, concerns, and issues that need to be understood from the client's frame of reference including religion, culture, identity development, and personal factors. The subjects of developmental stages of Muslims and their counseling issues are of enormous magnitude and require a whole new set of studies and publications, which I hope to present in the future.

Diversity within Unity

The following factors, among many others, make Muslims the most diverse of communities in the world.

Cultural Variations

Areas and regions that are known now as Muslim countries or countries with significant majority Muslim populations were not, in fact, void of cultures and heritage prior to Islam. On the arrival of Islam, whether it was through military conquest or as result of interaction through trade, cultures that predated Islam did not just disappear. Islam, instead, was absorbed and woven into the cultures, thus creating a unique fabric for each and every particular region of Islam.

Many customary practices have become incorporated into the religion of Islam and thus became almost inseparable from it. Esposito (1998), for instance, writes, "Nothing illustrates more the interaction of Qur'anic prescription and customary practice than the development of the veiling (hijab, burqa, or chador) and seclusion (purda, harem) of women in early

Islam. Both are customs assimilated from the conquered Persian and Byzantine societies. The Qur'an does not stipulate veiling or seclusion. On the contrary, it tends to emphasize the participation and religious responsibility of both men and women in Society" (p. 98). Although some Islamic traditional schools of thought or institutions may argue that Qur'anic stipulations support veiling, the different forms of veiling take on cultural forms. Esposito's argument of the ability of culture to blend with religion is true beyond dispute in many other forms of religio-cultural practices.

Nasr (1981) also explains.

Islamic history presents several instances in which foreign ideas have intruded within the world view of Muslim civilization, ideas which have in more than one instance been secular ... the first set of historical circumstances in the career of Islam concerned the Arab environment in which Islam was revealed. There were many pagan Arabian practices and traditions such as blood feuds, absolute allegiance to the tribe, and cults of idol worship which were banned in the universal perspective of Islam. Islam waged a battle against many such elements. (p. 9)

Geertz (1968) writes, "Our problem, and it grows worse by the day, is not to define religion but to find it" (p. 1). In comparing Morocco and Indonesia both religiously and culturally, Geertz (1968) states, "Their most obvious likeness is, as I say, their religious affiliation; but it is also, culturally speaking at least, their most obvious unlikeness" (p. 4). Confusing Islam and culture often results in conflicts among Muslims themselves who, on the one hand, share religious beliefs and, on the other, differ culturally. Lang (1997) states,

Islam is a powerful force in the immigrants' homeland, where over time, religion and culture have become fused. Thus each immigrant is likely to view his/her particular culture's understanding and application of Islam as the truest expression of the faith and to be uncomfortable with the Muslim perspectives that differ from these. (p. 102)

A specific example may, in fact, give clarity to this point. While the recently liberated central Asian republics (Turkmenistan, Uzbekistan, Kazakhstan, Kyrgyzstan, Tajikistan, and Azerbaijan), which gained their independence from the iron fist of the former Soviet Union, are looking to find their place in the Muslim world, they have two main concerns: first to help them reinforce local identity in the process of nation building and second to bridge European/Russian cultures with that of Asian Islam (Fuller, 1997). While cultures enjoy the general characteristics of their regions (e.g., Africa, Asia, and Europe), each culture is endowed with specific features that make it unique in both heritage and experience. An observer can easily note this by comparing, for instance, Indonesia with

Malaysia. While geographically they are situated in close proximity, they have vast differences in their understanding as well as applications of Islam.

On the issue of the role of women, for instance, Indonesia is considered more religiously liberal, while it is less tolerant of minorities than its neighboring Malaysia. Most interesting, both cultures attribute their practices to Islam.

Therefore, cultural variations of the Muslims in the world have a direct bearing on the way they practice Islam. Similarly, they may vary to a great extent in the way they view and consequently evaluate counseling and other mental health professions.

Nationalism

Unlike the parts of the world where national identities are often based on ethnic, racial, and historically shared values, in the Muslim world they are constructed mainly by the nation-state system (Khan, 1998). The Kuwaitis, the Saudis, and the Iraqis, for instance, have more shared values, yet they are maintained as different nationalities. On the contrary, Arabs and non-Arabs in Sudan and Arabs and Berbers in Algeria may have little to share; they are maintained as one nationality in each country. Emerging national identities provided new loyalties and affiliations for Muslims that became essential elements of how Muslim individuals view themselves, their society, and the world.

Religious Sectarianism

Farah (1994) states,

The overwhelming majority of Muslims today subscribe to Islam of the *sunnah* or *sunni* Islam with its faithful adherence to the doctrine evolved in the nascent Medinan period of Islam under the four orthodox caliphs. Subscribers to this doctrine are known as orthodox, or Sunni, Muslims. They constitute over 85 percent of the entire Muslim community today. All Sunnis are considered one sect, although juridically they subscribe to one of the four recognized rites or schools of thought (*madhahib*, sing. *madhhab*): Maliki, Shafi'i, Hanafi, or Hanbali. An adherent may pass from one into the other without ceasing to be known as an orthodox or Sunni Muslim. (p. 170)

The enforcement of a particular *madhhab* in a Muslim country may be referred to the religious authority, as in most of the Muslim world, or to the religious authority supported by the government, as in Iran and Saudi Arabia.

Although the differences between the four orthodox *madhahib* are minimal, this issue, coupled with cultural factors and nationalistic tendencies, has created deep divisions among the mainstream Muslim populations in the United States and, in fact, worldwide.

The second-largest sect after Sunni is Shiite, which constitutes from 10 to 15 percent of the world's Muslims, and according to Farah (1994) they constitute 14 percent. The Sunni-to-Shiite ratio in the United States is the same as that of the world. Division between Sunnis and Shiites occurred early in the Muslim history over the issue of the succession of the Prophet Muhammad. While Sunnis select the caliph from the community, Shiites limit the leaders, called Imams, to members of the family of the Prophet. Fisher (1997) explains,

Shiites are ardently devoted to the memory of Muhammad's close relatives; Ali, Fatima (the prophet's beloved daughter), and their sons Hasan and Husain. The martyrdom of Husayn at Karbala in his protest against the alleged tyranny, injustice and oppression of the Umayyad caliph is held up as a symbol of struggle against human oppression. (p. 348)

In addition to the political leadership, Shiites attribute to the Imam the quality of transmission of divine guidance, which is limited only to prophets in the Sunni tradition.

Shiites are further divided into sects, the largest of which is called the "Twelver" because the number of their Imams is twelve. The only country in which they exist as a majority is Iran. While they constitute a majority in Iraq, they live as a minority. They also exist as a minority in countries like Lebanon, Pakistan, and Saudi Arabia, to mention only a few. Other Shiite groups include the Isma'ilis and Seveners, which Sunni Muslims consider offshoots and often do not recognize as Muslims.

Aside from the issue of succession to the Prophet, Sunni and Shiites are in agreement on most issues of faith. Both perform the same essential religious practices and subscribe to the same moral values and principles. To illustrate, in areas where Shiites constitute a large community, they build their own houses of worship, institutions, and school systems. When they are not, they join the Sunni Muslims at the nearest Islamic institution to them for their worship, celebrations, and services. In the United States, there are large Shiite communities in several major cities (e.g., Los Angeles and Detroit). Large Shiite communities prefer to establish their own institutions to fulfill their religious, educational, and social needs. In other U.S. locations, Shiites join Sunni Islamic centers, send their children to Sunni Islamic schools, and seek to meet their religious needs through the services of local Sunni Islamic centers.

Other factors, such as language, history, geographic location, economic status, political structure, experience of colonialism, and the level of contacts with the outside world, particularly in European countries, also have produced influences in shaping both the understanding and the practices of Islam in a way unique to each particular country. This is not to mention the racial and ethnic divides that are evident and, at the same time, natural for the world of Islam, whose membership is not limited to a particular racial or ethnic group. The level of understanding and devotion may also further differences within the one sect, thus creating subgroups. These divisions and subdivisions are often misunderstood, underscored, and possibly unrecognized by both Muslims and non-Muslims, thus leading to the treatment of Muslims as only one way and one people.

In the following section, I present a brief summary of major beliefs and main characteristics of each of the most well known of the groups within the world Muslim community, including the mainstream Sunni Muslims and those described as offshoots. The purpose of such a summary is to provide an illustration of the wide range of groups among Muslims while, at the same time, avoiding overwhelming the reader with many of the historic, doctrinal, and philosophical details that could be addressed in a different type of literature for those who seek to deepen their knowledge about a particular area. This section, however, suffices for professionals who need this type of information to improve their competence in effectively dealing with Muslims.

Sunnis.

1. Forms the mainstream Islamic group.
2. Adopts the Qur'an and Sunna (Prophet's tradition) as primary sources of law.
3. Believes that leadership of the community after the death of the Prophet was legitimately transferred to the four rightly guided successors named caliphs and that such positions are a community's affair and choice.

Main Characteristics

1. Represents majority (i.e., 80–85 percent) of the world's Muslim population.
2. Forms the predominant majority population in most Muslim countries.
3. Exist as a minority in Iran, Lebanon, and Iraq, representing approximately 50 percent of the population in Iraq. (Although they may be equal or less in number to the Shiites, they have been in control of key positions in the Iraqi government since independence.)
4. Includes four different schools of thought that are called *madhahib* (the plural of *madhhab*).
5. Regards differences between these *madhahib* as variation of interpretations intended to allow for more inclusion and accommodation of different circumstances and situations, thus granting legitimacy to all of them. Only a small minority of Muslims in the world demand complete loyalty to their own schools of thought, thus disregarding others as less credible or even invalid. Muslims from various school of thought and various national origins can, therefore, worship together, establish family relations and business partnerships, intermarry, and share all aspects of life without being affected by such differences.

Islamic Schools of Thought (Madhahib).

1. H̄anafite
   a. The oldest of all four schools of thought.
   b. Founded on the principles of jurisprudence of Imam Abu Hanifa (d. 767).
   c. Known as Hanafi.
   d. Followed throughout the Muslim world, particularly in Turkey, India, Pakistan, Central Asia, and parts of the Arab world.

2. Malikite
   a. The second in historical order following the Hanafite.
   b. Established by Imam Malik bin Anas (d. 795).
   c. Known as Maliki.
   d. Started in Medina, Saudi Arabia.
   e. Followed throughout the Muslim world, mainly in northern Africa and other African countries.

3. Shafi'ite
   a. The third in historical order following the Malikite.
   b. Formed by Imam al-Shafei'i (d. 820).
   c. Known as Shafei'i.
   d. Followed throughout the Muslim world, mainly in Malaysia, Indonesia, Egypt, and Syria.

4. H̄anblite
   a. The fourth in historical order following the Shafi'ite.
   b. Founded by Imam Ahmad bin Hanbal (d. 855).
   c. Known as Hanbali.
   d. Followed mainly in Saudi Arabia.

Shiites.

1. Adopts the concept of *Imamat* as an additional article of faith, which means extending the religious authority to the Prophet's family after his death starting with his cousin and son-in-law Ali, followed by his sons and descendents.

2. The name Shi'ites means the partisans of Ali. While the Imamat has ended to various Shiite groups at different times depending on their belief, the loyalty to religious leadership and authority remains.

3. Employs esoteric understanding of the religion's texts, thus leading to the development of several traditions, all of which have sprung from Shiism. Esoteric understanding refers to the approach to doctrine that "looks beyond the outward manifestation, insisting that the apparent (zahir) is merely a camouflage of the true inner meaning, which is purposely hidden from the noninitiates" (Farah, 1994, p. 176).

Main Characteristics

1. Forms the second-largest group (i.e., 10–15 percent) of the world Muslim community after the Sunnis.

2. Makes up the overwhelming majority of Iran and approximately 50 percent or more in Iraq.
3. Exists as significant minorities in each of Yemen, Pakistan, Saudi Arabia, Bahrain, and Lebanon.
4. Provides the basis for many different Shiite groups that either have little in common, do not agree, or hardly recognize each other as religiously valid.

Shiite Subsects.

Ithna 'Ashriyyah (Twelvers)

- Represents the main body of Shiites.
- Believes in succession of twelve imams where the twelfth imam known as Muhammad is believed to have disappeared in 878 A.D. in the cave of the great mosque of Samarra' in Iraq, and until today Shiites expect his return. Therefore he's been called "Al muntazar," meaning "the awaited imam."
- Sanctions Mut'ah marriage, which is temporarily contracted marriage. This marriage is illegal in the Sunni tradition as well as some other Shiite traditions (e.g., Zaidis).
- Differs from Sunni Muslims, in addition to doctrinal and political differences, in the practice of some religious rituals (e.g., prayers), interpretation, as well as customs of some religious holidays. For instance, the day of 'Ashura, the 10th of the first month in the Islamic calendar called Muharram, is celebrated by both Sunni and Shiites for two different reasons and using different ways. Sunni Muslims celebrate the occasion as a form of gratitude to Allah for saving Prophet Moses and the Jews from the hands of the Egyptian Pharaoh (which is known in the Jewish tradition as Passover); Shiites celebrate the same day to commemorate the martyrdom of Imam Husain, the grandson of the Prophet and the second in their line of succession. Sunni Muslims celebrate the occasion by fasting that day, and making some sweet dishes the day before or after to share with relatives, friends, and neighbors; Shiites celebrate the same occasion by mourning, gathering, wailing, beating their chests, and, in extreme cases, causing injury to themselves in an attempt to relive the pain and suffering Imam Husain lived through before his death.

Zaidis

- They are the closest to Sunnis among Shiites and take their name from Imam Zaid, the grandson of Imam Husain.
- The exact number of the group is unknown although it is believed to have reached several millions.
- While they agree with Shiites on the concept of Imamat, they side with the Sunnis in rejecting Mut'ah marriages.
- A large number of Zaidis live in Yemen.

Ismai'lis

- Although they sprang originally from Shiites, neither group tolerates the other's beliefs or practices.

- They honor seven imams in the line of succession, in which the seventh (Ismai'l) died in 760 A.D. Hence they are called Ismai'lis and seveners.
- They believe in seven principles that are, according to Farah (1994): "(1) God; (2) the universal mind ('aql); (3) the universal soul (nafs); (4) primeval matter; (5) space; (6) time; (7) the world of earth and man" (p. 176). The meaning of these concepts is not well defined or understood in the same way to members of the group, let alone to outsiders.
- Due to their esoteric interpretation of Islam called "batini," implying a hidden meaning of the religion, they do not practice the most well-known Islamic religious practices such as prayers, fasting, and pilgrimage physically and outwardly as they are practiced by most Muslims around the world.
- Due to their small number, they attempt to proselytize and recruit new members.

Nusairis ('Alawites)

- Their belief sprang originally from Isma'ili Shi'sim.
- They revere Ali as god.
- They number less than half a million people.
- They are present mainly in Syria and control the presidency and most key governmental positions.
- They pose as Muslims while being rejected by all other groups including Shiites, thus barring intermarriages and attendance at religious gatherings.

Druzes

- Named after al-Darazi (d. 1019), who was appointed as a missionary by the Caliph al-'Hakim, who was known for his persecution of Orthodox Muslims, Jews, and Christians.
- Worship al-'Hakim (d. 1021) as god and express loyalty to al-Darzi.
- They believe in the six commandments of their faith which include: "(1) being sincere; (2) devotion to coreligionists; (3) expressing horror at paganism; (4) never having recourse to the devil; (5) believing in the unity of al-'Hakim; and (6) with eyes closed, submitting in heart and soul to his will" (Farah, 1994, p. 181).
- They believe that al-'Hakim will return to judge all on the Day of Judgment.
- They are present mainly in Syria, Lebanon and Israel.

Other Groups Identifying with Islam.

Kharijites

- The name Kharijities means "those who exited," thus referring to the early followers of Ali, the Prophet's cousin (the fourth caliph for Sunni Muslims and the first in line of succession for Shiites), who broke away from him during his leadership between 656 and 661 A.D.
- They adopt literal and extreme interpretation of the Qur'an and Hadith.
- Express harsh treatment to opponents, particularly other Muslims.

- They provide the ideological foundation for modern time's extremists.
- To them major sins are incompatible with faith.
- The early group believed in equality for women.
- They pursue strict, harsh, and poor lifestyles.
- While they are frowned upon by the Sunni Muslims, members of this group are not considered to be outside the folds of Islam because they follow the basic tenants of the faith and practice the pillars of Islam.

Qadianis or Ahmadiyyah

- They follow a reformer named Mirza Ghulam Ahmad from the Qadian city in the Punjab province of India, who appeared in the nineteenth century and claimed that he was the promised Messiah and later that he was a prophet of Allah who received divine revelation.
- Although they still follow the Qur'an, they adopted a new interpretation that provides foundation for their beliefs and practices.
- They are active in proselytizing and recruiting for the purpose of increasing their membership.
- A major split has occurred between members of the group; and one group is moving closer to the Sunni Islam tradition.
- Muslim scholars from the Sunni as well as Shiite traditions consider this group to be outside the folds of Islam and that their leader was a false prophet.

The Nation of Islam

- Established in the United States in the 1930s.
- Teaches superiority of the black people as the original inhabitants of the earth and creators of early world civilizations, and that God appeared as black man. That man was Wallace Fard Muhammad who claimed to be a prophet from Mecca, Saudi Arabia, while others suggest that he was a convicted felon who was just released from prison. Upon his disappearance in 1934, Elijah Poole became known as Elijah Muhammad and claimed the status of divine representative of God and his prophet.
- Encourages discipline, responsibility, pride in the black race, and family values.
- Flourished in the 1960s; Malcolm X appeared as the prominent spokesperson of the Nation.
- After the death of Elijah Muhammad and until today, the movement has been led by Minister Louis Farrakhan.
- Malcolm X was a member and a spokesperson of the Nation of Islam but changed his views of the Nation and of Islam when he went to pilgrimage in Saudi Arabia.
- Many Muslims resent the name of Nation of Islam and hence call it "Farrakhanism."
- Muslim scholars from both the Sunni and Shiite traditions consider the Nation

of Islam to be out of the folds of Islam completely due to their contradiction to the main beliefs, values, and practices of Islam.

- Elijah's son, Imam W. Deen Mohammed, established the Muslim American Society and.attempted to steer many of the former Nation of Islam members towards the mainstream Islam.
- There have been reports of Louis Farrakhan's attempts to reconcile differences, eliminate racist views, and move closer to the mainstream Islam.

As explained in other parts of this book, all people who describe themselves as Muslims pull together politically, economically and socially to some level during times of crisis, thus overlooking their religious differences. On the other hand, most members of groups that are outside the mainstream Sunni tradition may not join together or with Sunnis in mosques except with members of their own group. Intermarriage, particularly among members of the offshoots and the Sunnis, is almost nonexistent, and if it exists, it causes many social disagreements and conflicts of families on both sides.

Gender Roles

The issue of gender roles continues to be a source of controversy in Muslim communities both in the United States and abroad. To better understand the source of this controversy, I find it necessary to provide a brief historic overview of the status of women in Islam as well as an illustration of the variation among many Muslim countries and cultures with respect to Muslim women.

The Qur'an establishes certain rights and guarantees for women. In the early centuries of Islam, women enjoyed these rights in various aspects of life, including religious, social, political, and economic. In that era, women's participation and influence on public life was evident and constituted the norm rather than the exception. According to the Qur'an, there is full religious equality between men and women, meaning that both are required to fulfill the basic duties of the faith and that both will be called to account for their deeds on the Day of Judgment. Women's rights granted to them in Islam were not available to women in other parts of the world at the time of the Qur'anic revelation or for centuries after. It was not until what Al-Faruqi (1988) describes as the "centuries of decline" of Islam, which began in the year 1250 and continued until the late nineteenth century, that the role and participation of women in Muslim society deteriorated. The deterioration occurred as a result of the Mongol (fierce nomads from the east) invasions of the Muslim world and the destruction of Baghdad (the capital of the Islamic caliphate) including the burning and drowning of all books in libraries and schools (Al-Faruqi, 1994). The negative effects of these events were not limited to social, civil, political, or economic aspects of women's participation. Rather, they included the communal practice of Islam, such as attendance at the mosque, which was accepted at the time of the Prophet Muhammad. Before long, this changed to the virtual seclusion of the vast majority of Muslim women. Consequently, the primary role of the Muslim woman has become, therefore, that of wife and mother living within the extended family in a patriarchal society with little if any concern or awareness of life outside of her home, let alone being involved in outside life.

The Islamic family law that regulates the rights and responsibilities of each member in the family is the most central to the Islamic law (Shari'a). Esposito (1982) calls the Islamic family law the "heart of the Shari'a" (p. x). An illustration of its importance to Muslims is the fact that, in most Muslim countries where Islamic laws have been replaced by modern Western legal codes, the Islamic family law remained in force to govern the lives of Muslims all over the world. In the United States and Europe, where the Islamic law is not part of the judicial system, as well as in secular Muslim countries that do not enforce Islamic family law (e.g., Turkey), Muslim individuals, regardless of their religiosity, still insist on adhering to the Islamic family law. They perform marriages, seek counseling and mediation for their family disputes, and initiate religious divorces at mosques and Islamic centers (Haddad & Lummis, 1987; Kobeisy, 1999a).

As an overview of some of the cultural roots and variations among Muslim communities with respect to this issue, oppression of women is a universal phenomenon that manifests itself in almost all cultures of the world, including those of modern and industrialized countries. To illustrate, until the present time, women in both Europe and the United States, the most advanced in the world today with respect to women's rights and equality, are still receiving less pay than their counterparts for the same jobs. Other forms of oppression in the modern world are also alive and well, but I will not mention them simply because they are beyond the scope of this work.

Historically speaking, oppression of women pre-dates even history itself. Many historic accounts provide detailed descriptions of ways in which women have been oppressed, ranging from complete dependence on male relatives to being burned with the cremation of the husband's dead body. Muslim countries are also influenced by past histories and cultural practices, including those that deal with women and oppress them. Many of the most progressive Muslim feminists advocate that the prevailing oppression of women in the Muslim world results from the patriarchal and cultural interpretation of Islam, not Islam itself (El Saadawi, 1995; Walther, 1995). Smith (1997) states, "Most [Muslim women] proclaim their belief that true Islam is not only not repressive but is in fact the way to their liberation" (p. 60). El Saadawi (1995), a physician and a writer who is known for active advocacy of women's causes in the Arab world, states, "Mohammad was very progressive. He spoke highly of women; he loved women. Sexual relations are very flexible in Islam" (p. 83). The common ground between extremists and movements of women's liberation is that women should not be treated as sex objects (El Saadawi, 1995; Mustikhan & Ansari, 1998). Having said that, it is obvious that the fear of advocates for women's liberation is caused mainly by Muslim extremist groups, for they introduce their oppressive policies and laws in the name of religion. This makes resistance to such laws not only impossible but also dangerous (Bennoune, 1995; El Saadawi, 1995; Smith, 1997).

With respect to customs and cultures, the Arab world and most Muslim countries are characterized as overwhelmingly patriarchal and patrilineal societies. Within the various cultures of the Arab world alone, there are great differences in the treatment of women both officially and culturally.

The covering of the whole body of Muslim women is overwhelmingly practiced in a few countries of the Muslim world, such as Saudi Arabia, Iran, Afghanistan, and some parts of Pakistan. Although this covering is called different names in different regions, such as veil, *Chador, burqa,* or *purqa˙*, the concept is the same. While El Saadawi (1995) connects veiling to times before Islam, Christianity, and Judaism as a direct result of "the evolution of slave society and with patriarchy: monogamy for women and polygamy for men" (p. 83), Al-Faruqi (1994) refers to it as Persian and Roman practices that pre-date Islam. This is explained by the fact that in cultures where the custom of veiling is enforced, women of other religious groups are also practicing the veiling. In fact, enforcing the veil, *purdah,* and *burku˙* is seen as a means of containing and silencing women to achieve control over them (Wadley, 1994). Having said that, it is also worth noting that among convert Muslim women in the United States, there is a growing trend of veiling. For example, a white American Muslim woman who recently converted to Islam filed a law suit against the motor vehicle department of the state of Florida for not allowing her to keep her veil on in the photo for her identification card.

Some other Muslim countries (e.g., Tunisia and Turkey) have legally banned veiling and even the wearing of head covering in public for female students, government employees, and public officials.

Female genital mutilation, known as circumcision, is widespread to various levels of severity in African countries but not in Saudi Arabia or any of the Gulf states.

The honor-killing tradition, where women are killed not only for committing adultery but even for the suspicion of showing any behavior that is related to sexuality for the fear that it may bring shame to the family is common in some Arab and South Asian countries. According to Islam, both men and women are required to be modest. The consequences for engaging in sexual relations outside marriage are the same for both men and women. To target only women and even kill them is neither Islamic nor humane.

While historic references of accounts of women's participation in the public, political, and even military affairs of the Muslim community during the life of the Prophet are abundant, Muslim groups in Kuwait are showing great resistance to women's participation in the Parliament.

In matrilineal societies, which are prevalent in Southeast Asia (e.g., Malaysia and Sri Lanka), women enjoy a relatively high level of autonomy and social advantage. These advantages do not constitute, however, "a mirror image of that of men in so-called patrilineal societies" (Stivens, 1996, p. 3). According to customary laws in matrilineal societies, women are the keepers of inheritance, enjoy frequent involvement in kin decision making, and enjoy extensive property rights. Furthermore, women's importance in the household is reflected by the fact that the man would move to the woman's village on marriage (Stivens, 1996). These advantages have their effects on the social as well as the economic life of Muslims living in these cultures. While women enjoy property ownership and economic independence, their husbands are moving away to towns to escape living with in-laws in houses that are owned by their wives (Stivens, 1996). In the matrilineal system, women's coercion to accept arranged marriages is almost nonexistent or rare. Cross-cousin marriage has almost ended. Polygamy is not acceptable culturally and, therefore, has been discredited. In both systems, however, the matrilineal as well as the patrilineal, it is still difficult for the woman to get a divorce without resorting to an exhausting legal fight.

These variations in gender roles in Muslim countries strongly suggest that the cultural origins of these practices appear to have a stronger influence on these societies than that of the religion.

At the official level, women are still bound by laws that are neither Islamic nor humane. They range from giving only men the right to end marriages to the prohibition of public and political participation. In Saudi Arabia alone, women are not allowed to drive cars. Some analysts suggested that allowing women to sit in the driver's seat symbolizes freedom and control for women, something that is hard for the male-dominated society to accept. This "Islamized" policy led women into the streets of Riyadh, the Saudi capital, in protest while driving cars without licenses. It is worth noting that the majority of Muslim scholars today disagree with the Saudi scholars in their opinion about women's right to drive their own vehicles. They assert that such a policy brings more harm than good for the whole society.

Although reforms in the status of women in Muslim societies were made at the end of the nineteenth century in Egypt by a Muslim cleric, Rifa't Rafi' Al Tahtaoui (d. 1873), who succeeded in the establishment of the first school for girls' education in 1870, the twentieth century witnessed the most remarkable changes in the status of women. Both governments and individuals have been attempting to bring women back into full participation in Muslim societies. There are, now more than ever before, increased opportunities for women in education as well as in the workplace. Smith (1997) states,

Throughout the twentieth century, as Muslims have sought to reclaim their predominance on the world scene, discussions have been held as to the ways in which women's participation in the public realm needs to be reclaimed. The basis for these discussions, beginning in Egypt at the end of the last century and current now in many areas of the Islamic world, is not women's right per se but rather the importance of providing for the active functioning of both halves of Muslim society for the good of the whole. (p. 62)

Changes in women's status include the areas of education, work, political participation, and reforms in traditional practices of Islamic family law. Women are stipulating in their marriage contracts conditions that guarantee them more freedom in marriage and in initiating divorce. In addition to an awareness of oppressive traditional roles and the necessity to change them, these changes have been promoted by, among other things, the education of women, the criticism by many westerners with respect to women's position in Muslim societies, economic demands that have pushed women to work for economic independence or for supporting the family, and modernization, which is increasingly manifesting itself in the Muslim world (Haddad & Lummis, 1987; Smith, 1997).

This should not lead one to think that progress in women's rights and participation in society necessarily means westernization. In fact, women themselves, while continuing to enjoy more opportunities toward equality, are asserting their Islamic identity. Haddad and Lummis (1987) state:

At the same time, especially in the last decade in much of the Islamic world, some Muslims have been moved to rethink the importance of the Muslim family as the bastion of Islamic values. Thus, what might appear to the Western outsider to be a return to the traditional "bondage" of women, evidenced in such things as the adoption of specifically Islamic dress by some, can in fact be interpreted as the self-conscious choice of certain Muslim women to identify with Islam and to assume the responsibility of educating the males and the children in their families in the basis of Islamic life. (p. 125)

The progress of women in various aspects of life has met great resistance and presented tremendous challenges. Haddad and Lummis (1987) describe both currents in the Muslim world with respect to women's issues (i.e., supporters and opponents) as "each strong with articulate advocates" (p. 125). Opponents reaffirm the importance of traditional practices of Islam and the necessity of women staying in the home for the sake of

Islamic society, but supporters perceive the current position of women as alien to Islam and argue for equal rights in the workplace as well as equal participation in the religious, social, and political aspects of life.

I must note, however, that Muslim countries vary to a great extent in the level of success in changing the status of women.

With the rapid spread of cultural globalization through various media, reforms are likely to grow stronger and faster. This change is not, however, without risk. Rather, it carries the risk of a stronger wave of resistance that may cause a setback in the women's rights movement, thus leading to further institutionalization and the spread of existing cultural practices or extremists' views. A third possibility is that, through globalization, East versus West would lose their most distinctive differences, thus leading to cultures that have more in common.

Implications for Counseling

Because Islam binds Muslims into one international community, Muslim individuals are likely to be impacted in the form of stress and anxiety by adversities affecting other Muslims in any part of the world. If the concern stems from an event or a tension that is taking place in the client's country of origin, the suffering could be more direct and personal. An illustration of this could be war, terrorism, mass transportation (e.g., airplanes and trains) tragedies, and natural disasters (e.g., earthquakes, floods, etc.).

The emergence of nationalism and new national identities in the Muslim world from the beginning of the twentieth century and beyond provided new identities and loyalties for Muslims in these countries in addition to their Islamic identity. These Muslim states are not always at peace with each other. Therefore, American Muslims may be affected by the tensions and conflicts taking place between their countries of origin and other countries. An illustration of this is the dispute between India and Pakistan, which could be the cause of a divide between members of these two communities. Such tension in the relationship between the two communities intensifies if business partnerships or employment are involved, thus resulting in claims of discrimination and prejudice.

The majority of American Muslim families are still seen in the United States as supporting traditional gender roles. Freedom to understand and practice Islam in the United States is gradually breaking the confusion between cultures with regard to Islam in other parts of the Muslim world and Islam in the United States, thus allowing for more rights for women in the family and more participation in society, including in Islamic centers. Economic survival or prosperity, helping children with their homework, and self actualization are forcing Muslim women to seek education and careers. Therefore, the role of Muslim women in the United States is evolving to one that neither belongs to oppressive cultural practices in the East nor to very liberal feminist attitudes in the West. Muslim women in the United States are attempting to create a new balance between personal freedoms, traditional roles, and the demands of time and society.

Religious sectarianism is the cause of tensions among Muslims of different sects. In addition to the attempt to assert the legitimacy of one's sect or group, there are many barriers to complete social, political, and economic interactions among members of different groups. This could inhibit intermarriages, economic collaboration, and social interactions among members of different groups. The divisions among different groups and sects are becoming blurry or nonexistent in the minds of new generations, thus allowing for more opportunities for interaction and intermarriages. This trend, however, is creating a new set of problems among extended family members.

Because of strong tendencies and support for individualism in the United States, social pressure is either weak, nonexistent, or could be easily circumvented. Second generation American Muslims of both immigrant and convert backgrounds are likely to have more freedom not to be influenced by social pressure exerted by their extended families or larger Muslim communities.

Muslims are very diverse among themselves because of ethnic, cultural, and religious differences. Furthermore, historic experiences, educational levels, economic status, political orientation, professional achievements, and religious sectarianism, among many others factors, enhance such diversity.

Counselors and mental health professionals need to be aware of this fact and not generalize Muslims as one homogeneous group that is made of identical individuals. Proper counseling of Muslims must be based on an accurate assessment of religiosity and the cultural, racial, socioeconomic, and educational backgrounds of the client.

Individual Muslims may adhere to religious instructions or cultural practices willingly and by choice. Counselors, therefore, must not mistake such adherence with oppression. To illustrate this confusion, many counselors may erroneously attribute the mental instability of a Muslim woman to her dress, religion, or culture. There are many examples, even in patriarchal cultures, in which some women are privileged and enjoy a great deal of freedom, responsibility, and even leadership roles. An Arabic proverb states, "While the man usually communicates the decision to other men, he does not tell who made the decision." Counselors should clearly separate their own preferences from those of their clients and not show a judgmental attitude. If a woman, for instance, is happy with the way she dresses, the counselor should not insist that it is a sign of oppression and must be changed. Furthermore, counselors should assess their clients' abilities and willingness so that clients are not dragged into battles that are those of the counselor, that are not their own, or that they are not ready for or willing to undertake.

AMERICAN MUSLIMS AND ISLAM IN AMERICA

By "American Muslims," I mean Muslim individuals and families for whom the United States constitutes the main or only homeland. This includes both converts and immigrants. There is no distinction drawn in this definition between recent and longtime immigrants or between forced refugees and free-choice opportunity seekers.

History and Demography

While Islam and Muslims in the United States are viewed mostly as foreign, the presence of Muslims goes back to the seventeenth century or even earlier. Pathe Diagne, a linguist and historian, contends that Africans discovered the navigational route from Senegal across the Atlantic in 800 B.C. He claims that they laid the basis for the Olmec civilization in what is now Veracruz, Mexico. He also maintains that he has evidence that, in 1312, more than 170 years before Columbus, an Islamic emperor in West Africa named Mansa Bakari II sailed to America with an expedition of 2,000 boats and settled there (*The Post Standard*, 1993, p. D10).

Another account links Muslims' presence in the United States to the slave trade. Bernstein (1993) reported, "Scholars argue that a portion of the West Africans who were brought to North America as slaves in the 17th and the 18th centuries may have been Muslims, though they lost the faith and it did not take roots among American blacks until recent times" (p. 3).

There are numerous accounts of Muslims brought to the West as slaves. The *American Muslim Journal* (July 8, 1994) reported an update on the May 1991 archeological discovery of the New York–African burial ground. The report estimated the burial time to have occurred in the beginning of the seventeenth century or even earlier. Among those found were African slaves buried in Muslim style. Estimates of the proportion of Muslims within the total numbers of African slaves brought to the Western Hemisphere range from 14 to 20 percent (Denny, 1995). According to Rashid (1990), "The inhumanity of chattel slavery, however, did not allow them to transmit Al-Islam to their children and their Islam ended with their passing" (p. 11).

The Muslims of North America can be divided into two distinct groups: immigrant Muslims and indigenous Muslims. According to Haddad and Lummis (1987),

In the first category are those who have come, or whose parents or grandparents have come, from other areas of the world to this country including the increasingly large number of students on college and university campuses. Originally mainly Lebanese, they now represent Islamic communities from more than sixty nations especially Pakistan, Iran, Afghanistan, Turkey, and Eastern Europe. The second category, that of so-called indigenous Muslims, is composed mainly of members of the African-American community of the United States, and now includes a growing number of "Anglo" converts (estimated up to seventy-five thousand). (p. 3)

As for the immigration of Muslims to the United States, it might have started as early as the nineteenth or late eighteenth century and occurred in several waves. The first wave occurred in the late 1800s and was mainly Arabs from greater Syria. Most of these people were poor and working class. They took American spouses and assimilated in American society. This wave continued until World War I, after which a second wave continued through the 1930s, ending with World War II (Denny, 1995; Haddad, 1986).

A third wave of Muslim immigration after World War II included many people from the elite of Middle Eastern and South Asian countries seeking education and professional advancement. Although many returned to their home countries, a large number remained. According to Denny (1995), "Members of this wave tended to keep their Islamic identity while assimilating into North American life at a moderate rate. These members are labeled by more observing Muslims as 'Eed 'ID' Muslims, because of their supposed habit of attending the mosque only during the two canonical religious festivals each year" (p. 297).

The emigration patterns reflected changes in American immigration policies as well as sociopolitical and economic upheavals overseas. Like other immigrants, Muslims represent a myriad of interests and goals. Their immigration was initiated in an effort to enjoy the benefits the United States provides: economic and social enhancement, political refuge, and religious freedom (Ahmed, 1991; Haddad, 1991; Nyang, 1991).

Estimates of the size of the Muslim population in the United States put the figure between four and more than eight million Muslims (*Almanac*, 1992; Cornell, 1990; Stone, 1991). The reason for such a gap is the lack of means by which to ensure an accurate membership count for the Muslim population. At any rate, many scholars predict that the Muslim population, because of immigration, high birthrates, and conversion, will become the second-largest religious group after Christians in a decade or so (Bernstein, 1993; Findly, 1992). Others declare that Muslims are the second-largest religious group already. The four-million estimate, however, dates back to 1980, so it is old and does not take into consideration demographic patterns leading to an amazingly rapid expansion of the Muslim population (Findly, 1992; Ostling, 1988; Stone, 1991). In fact, news alerts by the Council on American Islamic Relations (CAIR), issued sometimes more than once a day, state that there are an estimated six to eight million Muslims in the United States.

While Muslims in any single Islamic country can be regarded as homogeneous both culturally and religiously, we find that Muslim minorities in the United States are very diverse and representative of the diversity of the world Muslim population. According to Stone (1991), based on ethnicity and country of origin, the breakdown of the 1980 estimate is as follows: "Indigenous African-American Muslims constituted over 30 percent of the Muslims living in America. Another 28.4 percent were Muslims from the Middle East/North Africa, while East Europeans comprised 26.6 percent of Muslims in the United States. The remaining proportion of Muslims was composed predominantly of Asians, 11.5 percent" (p. 28). The remaining number comes from the Caribbean, sub-Saharan Africa, and other parts of the world. Haddad and Lummis (1987) reported more than six million Muslims in the United States, of which 12.4 percent are Arab, 42 percent are African American, 24.4 percent are Asian, and 21 percent are "other" (cited in Hedayat-Diba, 2000). These proportions might have changed to a great extent because of new world events, such as the influx of refugees from Bosnia in the former Yugoslav republic in Europe, as a result of ethnic cleansing, and with the regulations limiting the immigration of males from most Muslim countries of the Middle East and Asia as a result of the September 11 terrorist attacks. If they have not, they soon will. According to Ba-Yunus and Siddiqi (1998), the distribution of ethnicity among American Muslims is as follows:

The people of Arab origin or their first and second generation descendants lead the pack with 32.7 percent, followed by American Muslims with 29.5 percent, most of whom understandably are of African American origin. Proportionately, South Asians from Pakistan, India, Bangladesh, Sri Lanka, Nepal, Maldives Islands, and Arakan constitute a very close third (29.3 percent). In the remaining .5 percent, most noticeable are Kurds, Albanians, and Bosnians as well as those from the West Indies and Latin America. (p. 32)

According to the American Muslim Council (1992), "the immigrant Muslims represent 56 percent while the indigenous make 44 percent of the total Muslim population." The ethnic distribution according to this study is as follows: "African American 42 percent, South Asians 24.4 percent, Arabs 12.4 percent, African 6.2 percent, Iranians 3.6 percent, Turks 2.4 percent, South East Asians 2.0 percent, American Whites 1.6 percent, other 5.6 percent" (p. 16). It also states that the immigrants represent 55 percent while the indigenous members represent 45 percent.

In conclusion, although historians have not agreed on who were the first Muslims to set foot in America in the seventeenth century, or where and when they did so, one can assert two facts with confidence: Muslims are here to stay, and they are numerous.

Figure 2.9 Ethnic origins of American Muslims according to Stone (1991)

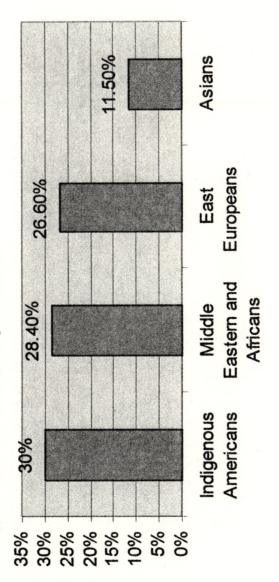

Figure 2.10
Ethnic distribution of American Muslims according to the American Muslim Council (1992)

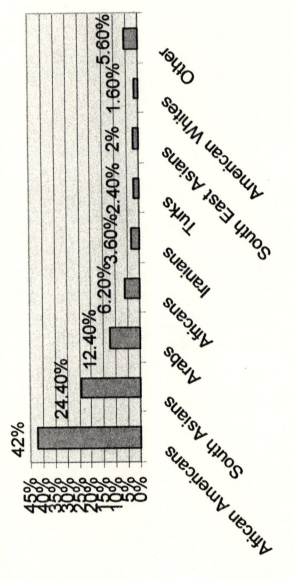

Figure 2.11
Ethnicity of American Muslims according to Ba-Yunus and Siddiqui (1998)

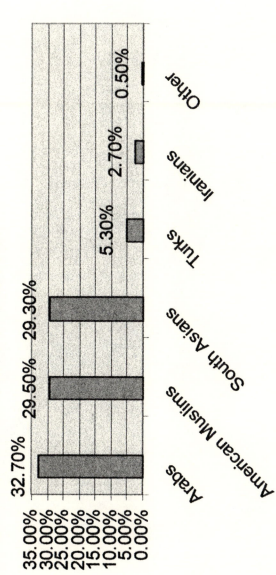

With the rapid increase in number of American Muslims, their mosques, full-time schools, and institutions are also expanding in size and services. In five years only, the number of mosques has doubled (Haddad & Lummis, 1987). Yet despite unmatched growth, Muslims' needs are far from being studied, let alone recognized and met (Haddad & Lummis, 1987).

Commonalities among American Muslims

Faith

Although American Muslims come from widely diverse cultural and ethnic backgrounds, they are drawn together by the religious beliefs and values they share. Goldman (1993) of the *New York Times* witnessed the opening ceremony of a mosque (*masjid*) and reported the following: "The Master of ceremony was a doctor from Kashmir. The call to prayer was chanted by a welder from Trinidad. The building's plans were done by an architect from Turkey, and the feast that followed the ceremony was prepared by a chef from East Pakistan. All are Muslims" (p. A1).

Through both immigration and conversion, diversity among Muslims in the United States is intertwined with that of the general population, as Marquand (1996a) noted: "The Country's diversity is creating multicultural Mecca for Muslims" (p. 1). Islam is, therefore, binding people together despite their differences.

Anti-Islam Biases

Many of the challenges that Muslims face are felt, although to varying degrees, by every Muslim regardless of their differences. Regular attacks on Islam and Muslims in the media and society have become commonplace. Ironically, these biases may have had religious origin. Farris (1992), while explaining how stereotypes against Middle Easterners including Muslims were introduced to him, said,

I had attended the First Baptist Church in Billings, Montana with my family. I had been taught in Sunday school and vacation Bible school that ancient Israelites were a force for good and the ancient Egyptians and Philistines were a force for evil. Perhaps it was difficult for my eight-year-old mind to realize that a few millennia can change things considerably. Many Christian fundamentalists continue to err by applying an ancient biblical scenario to the present day Middle East. (p. 40)

Academia, itself being not immune to the anti-Islamic biases, has aided the propagation of inaccuracies. The media comes a close second, coupled with political institutions. Edward Said (1981) explains this quite eloquently by saying,

The orthodox coverage of Islam that we find in the academy, in the government, and in the media is all interrelated and has been more diffused, has seemed more persuasive and influential in the West than any other "coverage" or interpretation. The success of this coverage can be attributed to the political influence of those people and institutions producing it rather than necessarily truth or accuracy. (p. 64)

Former Vice President Dan Quayle's remark in his address to West Point's graduating class of 1992, "I must also take this opportunity to caution you that my own personal fear, and indeed the fear of most of the civilized world, is the rising Islamic fundamentalism." William Baker, chair of Christians and Muslims for Peace, attacked the Western media portrayal of Islam and described Quayle's words concerning Islam as "an American policy being expressed." He added, "Why is Jerry Falwell not dangerous to the world, and why is a 'Christian fundamentalist' not a threat to any one in the West?" (cited in Bhatt, 1994, p. 1).

In a column titled "U.S. Culture and Fundamentalist Islam Don't Mix," Buckley (1993) suggested reforms in the immigration laws that exclude Muslims from coming to the United States. He asserts, "So we are going to have to take explicit notice of the incompatibility of our own culture and that of the fundamentalist Muhammmedans, and we need to organize our immigration laws with some reference to this problem" (p. 8). Sensational and inflammatory headlines such as "Islam Is a Religion from Hell" are becoming increasingly familiar (Bhatt, 1994). They are also damaging and harmful. While such statements lead to hate crimes and outright discrimination against Muslims, they also affect Muslims' self-image and may lead to hostility toward society.

Khan (1998) states,

This attitude that Islam is a major threat to the West in the post-communist era alienates many American Muslims, putting them on the defensive and creating barriers that discourage their assimilation. Many American experts and scholars often fail to distinguish between accepting Muslims and accepting Islam. America will continue to alienate its Muslim population as long as it continues to demonize Islam each time it faces resistance to foreign objectives in Muslim states or from Muslim movements. (p. 117)

What is described as the first national survey on attitudes toward and among minorities was released on March 2, 1994. The survey of 2,755 people showed that every group surveyed believed Muslims to belong to a religion that condones violence, is anti-American, and oppresses women. Harris, the surveyor, believes that this sort of rigid categorization is fed by the shorthand portrayal of minorities offered by television and other mass media as well as through confrontation that awakens prejudice. Such feelings and attitudes have intensified after the September 11 terrorist attacks.

Furthermore, Hollywood's film industry often portrays Muslims as dark, sinister, and uneducated bedouins who come from the Third World, the Middle East. At the same time, they portray Jesus as a white blond-haired and blue-eyed man, ignoring the fact that he was Middle Eastern.

The media uses terms such as "Islamic" to link acts of terrorism to Islam, while displaying the greatest deal of sensitivity and delicacy when dealing with similar acts done by Jews and Christians. This is seen by Muslims as demonization of Islam and alienation of Muslims. Khan (1998) states, "These media tactics not only set public opinion against Islam and American Muslims but lead to hate crimes against them, and encourage the belief among American Muslims that America is antagonistic to Islam" (p. 117).

Muslims in the United States are also perceived as people who are resistant to change, integration, and modernity and who do not like to live with others or be joined by others. Bernstein (1993) reported, on the contrary, "In the major centers of Islamic life, from Los Angeles to New York with stops in between, most Muslims say that they are far from anti-American. Indeed, they are concerned that a tiny number of extremists could tarnish the reputation of the vast majority, and they are angry at news and entertainment media that, they believe, are too quick to portray Islam as a religion of fanatics" (p. 26). In the same article, Abu Khalil of the Middle East Institute is quoted saying, "If the question is, 'Are there kooks among the Muslims?' Of course there are, he said, and we should be entitled to have our share of zealots and kooks. But there is the same diversity of view point and life style among Muslims as there is among other groups" (p. 26). Bernstein added, "Many Muslims here are not nearly as concerned with international politics as with issues of morality, religion and daily life" (p. 26).

Muslims are concerned for the well-being and the development of the societies in which they live. "We want to be part of the Mosaic. We don't consider ourselves to belong to the Middle East or to South Asia. Our roots are there but our present and our future are here," a Dr. Hathout said to Bernstein (1993). Haddad (1991) also notes, "American Muslims are experiencing both exhilaration at the opportunity to increase their numbers and develop their institutions and frustration and dismay as they continue to experience prejudice, intimidation, discrimination, misunderstanding and even hatred" (p. 3).

By limiting their coverage of the Muslim world to "violence and upheaval, the media create the impression that these calamitous events are the rule rather than the exception of daily life in the region. The American media provide the public with very little evidence to contradict that widely held yet baseless assumption" (Noakes, 1998, p. 370). These images have led to a great deal of oppression for Muslim children in schools

(Wormser, 1994) and for Muslim individuals in places of employment as well as in public places.

This portrayal of Islam and Muslims has led American Muslims to find ways to combat these views and images. One of the ways is to participate in public welfare by volunteering to help victims of natural disasters and sheltering and feeding homeless and poor people (Wormser, 1994). They are also joining in interfaith and public forum discussions and even initiating campaigns to express Muslims' stands on issues. Muslims in the United States have established various national organizations that are characterized as inclusive and representative of all American Muslims. One of these organizations is the American Muslim Council, which seeks to empower Muslims politically regardless of their religious affiliations (Khan, 1998). Another example is CAIR, the main purpose of which is to follow up on cases of discrimination and civil rights injustices against Muslims and resolve them. CAIR was established also to help improve the Muslim image. It publishes an annual report on the status of Muslims' civil rights. The first report was titled "A Rush to Judgment" and was published following the Oklahoma City bombing. Although many Muslims were skeptical about the change that organizations such as CAIR could bring, support grew rapidly after success stories demonstrating CAIR's effectiveness in numerous cases of stereotyping and discrimination.

Pulling together to fight the battle against prejudice is what Khan describes as "indulging in identity politics" (p. 117). Khan (1998) explains,

Thus, in a way the demonization of Islam by the American media compels Muslims to indulge in identity politics. They concentrate on defending their faith from a perceived American assault rather than on their role as American residents seeking liberty, equality, and prosperity. The negative image of America, a consequence of its foreign policy in the Middle East, inspires a paradoxical response from Muslims. Its prosperity and freedom attracts them, but once they're here, its policies and attitudes towards Muslims and Islam alienates them. The result is a dilemma for American Muslims: they like living here but they love to hate America. (p. 117)

This can also lead to more consciousness of a sense of community and religious obligations. To illustrate, a number of immigrants had never gone to a mosque before being in the United States and had previously believed that adherence to particular Islamic teaching is not a crucial issue. This attitude has changed in the United States, as Haddad and Lummis (1987) describe: "Many have actually found their consciousness about their religious identity enhanced in the American context as people question them about the basic tenets of their religion. They are also intrigued by media reports and are perplexed as to why Western society and the press seem to fear Islam and Muslims. Many students report that they have become committed to their faith after a search for roots in the American context" (p. 22).

Challenges for the Muslim Identity

Muslim minorities struggle within their larger societies to survive the challenges of assimilation and protect their cultural and religious heritage—something characteristic of minorities. One of these challenges is how to live Islamic life in a non-Muslim country (Voll, 1991). As explained earlier, by dint of the diverse backgrounds of Muslims, many voices may rise within a single Islamic organization expressing various understandings of Islam.

Strengthened by a sense of survival of faith and culture, Muslims tend to overcome their differences. This leads Muslims of various sectarian backgrounds (e.g., Sunnis, Shiites, and Sufis) to go to the same mosque, send their children to the same weekend or full-time Islamic school, celebrate together, and bury their loved ones in the same cemetery. Furthermore, while not accepted by the mainstream as true Muslims because of ideological differences, groups that affiliate themselves with Islam (e.g., Qadianis and Nation of Islam members) may overcome their differences and unite with Muslims.

In Islamic organizations, the tendency to enforce the most conservative culture advocated, even if only a minority of its members support it, is much greater than the tendency to reach a middle ground. This attitude occurs because, as Lang (1994) states, "Muslims prefer to err on the conservative side" (p. 102). Opposition to such rigid, conservative cultural interpretations of Islam is often dismissed as Western influenced and, hence, un-Islamic. It is similarly important to note that most of the new converts to Islam do not noticeably influence the policies or the applications of Islam. Rather, they hasten to change their names to Arabic ones and even start wearing Arabic costumes, assuming that they are religious obligations. In contrast, the Prophet occasionally wore outfits that were not Arabian and allowed men from Ethiopia (e.g., Bilal) and Persia (e.g., Salman) to keep their names (Lang, 1997).

What brings all these people together is their common cause against outside pressure and felt animosity. Their Islamic identity is bombarded on a daily basis by stereotypes in schools, in the workplace, and in neighborhoods (Haddad, 1991; Haddad & Lummis, 1987; Nyang, 1991; Voll, 1991). Furthermore, Muslim identity is negatively affected by U.S. foreign policies dealing with the Muslim world (Haddad, 1991). Haddad (1987) states,

This identity is clarified and molded daily by the treatment Muslims receive in their places of residence and employment, in the schools and by the courts. It is altered and negotiated repeatedly as a result of the discrimination they experience as they deal with the images projected about them by the host society in literature, the movies, and the media. And in a very dramatic way, it has been shaped during the last four decades by the vagaries of foreign American policy in the Middle East and America's relations with Muslim countries throughout the world. (p. 15)

Peer pressure has also been cited as a main influence in the lives of young people. Wormser (1994) describes the account of Nathmia, a 14-year-old Muslim girl, saying,

When fourteen-year-old Nathmia Turki went to school on the morning of February 1, 1990, she was not aware that something was different. A few students gave her funny looks, as usual. Being a second-generation Muslim teenager from the Middle East in an American public school in the South had never been easy for Nathmia. Covering her head with a hejab (scarf) made things even more difficult. But except for a few half-joking, half-obnoxious remarks, she never had any serious problems. She had even managed to make a few good friends. But as Nathmia opened her locker that February morning, someone suddenly slammed into her, smashing her against her locker.

"Go back where you belong, you dirty Arab," someone shouted at her and then spit and ran down the hall. Later, when Nathmia was seated in the principal's office, she learned that the United States had just bombed Iraq. (p. 3)

On the one hand, Muslims in the United States appreciate freedom and enjoy the opportunity, economic and otherwise. On the other hand, they do not like what they consider an excess of freedom for the fear of undermining Islamic religious principles.

These factors may cause a love–hate relationship that affects Muslims' attitudes in accepting or rejecting what is available in American culture, not necessarily on a religious basis. They feel they want the opportunity the United States offers while, at the same time, rejecting several forms of American lifestyles. Furthermore, they are greatly influenced by the domestic as well as the foreign policies of the United States.

To conclude, American Muslims find themselves facing two major challenges: the widespread anti-Islam bias and the danger of melting into the American pot and thus losing their Islamic identity. As a result, they have had to stick to their common ground and overlook their differences.

From a sociopsychological point of view, this is to be expected, although sometimes people identify with the powerful forces of society and attempt to reflect their new group when experiencing prejudice. This is likely to intensify the identity crisis for Muslims. Figure 2.12 shows general patterns of identity formation among American Muslims, both immigrants and indigenous.

Diversity among American Muslims

Ethnic and Racial Diversity

On the one hand, as much as barriers of racial and ethnic differences are suppressed, they remain a major part of the most influential obstacles to Muslims' unity. On the other hand, this unity may be for economic

Figure 2.12
Patterns of identity formation among American Muslims

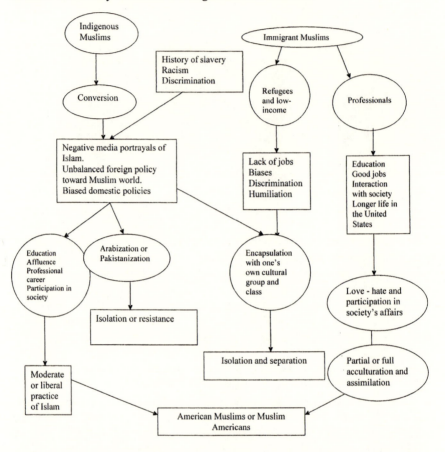

reasons rather than religious ones. Research suggests that when such groups acquire membership sufficient for supporting their own institutions, they split in an effort to stay away from other groups. Describing the ethnicity- or nationality-based mosques, Haddad and Lummis (1987) state, "In addition to being places of worship, they function as social centers and organizing units providing cohesion to national groups and the comfort of a common cultural and linguistic identity. It is also true that in some cases the mosque may be the only avenue available for positions of leadership in society, giving added significance to the maintenance of a distinctive minority status" (p. 38).

Socioeconomic Factors

The Muslim population in the United States is formed mainly by two major groups: indigenous people who are mainly African Americans, and immigrants. Division among these two groups is reinforced by cultural and socioeconomic differences. Many of the immigrants are physicians, engineers, and businesspeople who reside in the suburbs and tend to assimilate quickly into American culture. African American Muslims, while they include professionals, tend to be concentrated in or around the inner city and are affected, to a great extent, by past and current experiences of racism. Immigrants are also divided by nationality and ethnicity, by differences in the groups to which they belong, and by the generation gap between more assimilated immigrants and new arrivals (Steinfels, 1993).

These differences, coupled with differences arising from affiliation with a particular school of thought or specific nationality, may lead a particular community, if they have sufficient resources, to establish their own mosques and institutions in order to worship according to their own traditional ways. On the issue of racism, many African Americans believe that in the Arab world, racism is still a serious problem (Wormser, 1994). They also believe that only members of their community are capable of understanding their concerns. Conard Muhammad, an African American, states, "Only a black man can really understand our culture. You have to know our ways in order to change the conditions of our people. No Arab alive can change the condition of the black man. Only those who know the black experience can do so" (cited in Wormser, 1994, p. 102).

The drop in the number of new immigrants from the Muslim world while, at the same time, American Muslims are dropping their ethnic particularities could lead in future generations toward a common Islamic identity (Haddad and Lummis, 1987).

Political Orientation

The differences over political priorities between African Americans and immigrants are evident. African American Muslims are concerned with local agendas and domestic policies in American politics. According to Conard Muhammad (Wormser, 1994), "The criteria for Muslims in Washington, DC, to establish themselves should not be much different from the criteria that Muslims in Texas, Montana, New York or Michigan would use to establish themselves" (p. 4).

Immigrant American Muslims are seen as being more concerned with U.S. foreign policies than they are with domestic policies (Haddad, 1991). Both immigrant and local Muslims are Republicans as well as Democrats, and members of each group are on both sides of most issues. The gap between the two groups is widened further by religious, ethnic, and cultural differences.

Changing Cultures

Muslims are undergoing a cultural shift in the United Stated in an attempt to cope with new and rapidly changing social, educational, and economic demands and conditions. While Muslim converts are struggling to adopt new practices from traditional Muslim cultures, immigrant Muslims are, to the contrary, struggling to fit into the mainstream American culture. Awareness of race and racial issues, the level of acculturation, age gaps, rapidly changing popular culture, and the level of adherence to religious values are among the factors that produce various cultures among Muslims of America. The functions, responsibilities, and rights of individuals, families, institutions, and those in charge of such institutions are being redefined.

Masajid in the United States are more than just places of worship as is the case in most Islamic countries. For Muslims, *Masajid* provide educational, social, and economic services in addition to religious ones. For other faiths, *Masajid* hold inter-religious dialogues, discussions about Islam, and functions of concern to the larger community. The role of imams (religious leaders) is also changing. Haddad and Lummis (1987) state,

> As is true with other aspects of the practice of Islam in the United States, the role of imam here often takes on dimensions not normally present in the Islamic world. . . . To some extent, this is due to the different circumstances in the United States. Demands for instruction in Islam, for "pastoring" to a congregation many of whose members may be having difficulties adjusting to a new culture, for visiting the sick and bereaved and providing family counseling, all press the imam to enlarge the scope of his functions. And, in this country, the absence of those other professionals to whom individuals might go for specialized services— shaykhs (religious leaders), qadis (judges), ʿalims (persons learned in law and theology)—means that these responsibilities are added to what is expected of an imam.
>
> The expansion of roles required of the North American imam is also due in part to the variety of activities engaged in by priests, pastors, and rabbis in their respective communities. Imams in some cities are asked to join ecumenical organizations, to speak at gatherings where presentations are also made by Christian and Jewish clergy, and to appear on local radio or TV programs to talk about Islam. (pp. 58–59)

Marquand and Andoni (1996b) also state, "Muslims today are not only adding to the multicultural identity of America, but they fashion their own form of worship in this country, they are developing new interpretations of Islam and way of living that could influence the practice of Islam—the world's fastest growing religion—elsewhere around the globe" (p. 9).

John Esposito, the director for the Center of Muslim-Christian Understanding at George Washington University, was quoted saying, "They are trying to do what every group has done—trying to assimilate, yet remain distinct" (cited in Marquand & Andoni, 1996b, p. 9). Forced assimilation, however, is not always easy or helpful.

Crollius (1984) states, "Our world knows many groups of people who live in a state of 'cultural schizophrenia,' becoming gradually alienated from their own culture without finding a home in the culture that pretends to absorb them" (p. 50). In addition to its negative impact on those assimilating, total assimilation deprives the hosting culture from the riches and originality of the cultures of those assimilating—Muslims in this case—and leads to what Crollius (1984) describes as "impoverishment of human values" (p. 50).

In the West in general and in the United States in particular, Muslims are living new experiences in societies characterized by social, economic, and political freedoms. This means changes and modifications of understanding as well as practicing religion and life on a daily basis. This includes but is not limited to changes in gender roles within the Muslim family.

Religious Affiliations

Muslims—and specifically Muslims in the United States—are not a monolithic group. All the world's Muslim religious divisions are represented in the United States. Muslims are divided religiously into at least two main groups: Sunni and Shiite. The latter constitutes 14 percent of the total number of the Muslim population in the United States and worldwide (Farah, 1994). The majority of indigenous American Muslims, mainly African Americans, who constitute 30.2 percent of the total Muslim population in the United States (Stone, 1991), identify themselves with mainstream Sunni Islam, while the rest of them constitute the membership of the American Muslim Mission led by Imam W. D. Muhammad. Muhammad diverted from his father's Nation of Islam and instructed his followers to integrate his community into the larger Muslim community (Ahmed, 1991, p. 20). In a recent development, Imam Muhammad resigned from the leadership of this community without the announcement of a replacement. In a news alert issued by the Council on American Islamic Relations (CAIR) on December 3, 2003, a new leader from New Jersey, Mustafa Al-Amin, has emerged and expressed his intentions to lead and integrate the group to mainstream Sunni Islam.

While most Muslims identify themselves as Sunni, there are also an Iranian Shiite group, 14 strains of black Muslims, and other offshoots, including mystical Sufism (Marquand & Andoni, 1996b). Many African American Muslims are affiliated with the Nation of Islam. According to Wormser (1994), Imam Talib Abdur-Rashid, of the Mosque of Islamic Brotherhood in New York, notes, "In the African-American community, we do not lightly dismiss the Nation of Islam. They are an important part of our history. Many Muslims in our community would not be there if it were not for the Nation. We respect them even though we have disagreements with them. They are important in the life of our people" (p. 104). Other Sunni Muslim officials have reasons to believe that the Nation of Islam is gradually moving toward mainstream Islam (Wormser, 1994, p. 103).

In summary, American Muslims are united by the Islamic faith and the external challenges facing them and divided internally by their ethnicity, socioeconomic standing, political ideology, cultural diversity, and religious orientation. The issue of religious divisions within the Muslim community is one of great importance since it has a direct bearing on the perception of its members and carries significant implications worth considering.

According to Haddad and Lummis (1987), "because North American Muslims have not yet developed anything like a theological institute and have little indigenous scholarly production, they are often dependent on current interpretations by Muslims from overseas as to what Islam is and how it should be practiced" (p. 158). In a survey to explore the universal and mental health values among Muslims in the United States, over three-quarters of the sample considered themselves quite religious. They were not, however, a completely homogeneous group by any means, as was shown by divided opinion on adherence to Islamic schools of law, sympathy for Sufism, and the relationship of human freedom and divine determination (Kelly, Aridi, & Bakhtiar, 1996, p. 216).

Implications for Counseling

The identity of American Muslim individuals is far more complex than being influenced only by Islam. Assessment of the person's individual characteristics (e.g., education, level of acculturation, profession, and experiences in the American society) and group affiliation (e.g., cultural or ethnic background, religious sectarian affiliation, national origin, history, and political status) will help counselors better understand their clients.

Because of various factors, most Muslims' view of the American mental health field and mental health professionals is negative, so that utilization of mental health services is unusual or rare. Within this context, it will be difficult to establish trust (Hedayat-Diba, 1999). This will require more time for professionals to establish rapport with their Muslim clients. To help in this respect, counselors need to acknowledge their awareness of the widespread stereotypes and misrepresentation of Islam and Muslims and assure their clients of both neutrality and positive regards and expectations. In order to deal with fears and suspicions, counselors need to illustrate to their Muslim clients the authenticity of their sources of information on Islam and demonstrate expertise by sharing previous experiences with cases involving Muslim clients and the success achieved in such cases without, of course, breaching the confidentiality of their former clients.

A general observation suggests that stages of racial and cultural identity models defined for and applied to other minority groups (e.g., Asian Americans) (Sue, 1989) including conformity, dissonance, resistance and immersion, introspection, synergetic articulation, and awareness, may be occurring with the Muslim identity development process to a similar or varying degree.

The challenge this process poses to the counselor is that with every stage, corresponding attitudes that the minority person exhibits must be taken into consideration and understood by the counselor. At the same time, I caution counselors from assuming that such processes are taking place without accurate assessment and understanding.

Because various groups are influenced by different factors, each ethnic and national group of Muslims may have its own ease or difficulty adjusting to the American culture. As Hedayat-Diba (1999) states, "Psychological theories may not be sufficiently culturally attuned to facilitate the development of 'biculturism'" (p. 312). Counselors must not hasten to blindly apply such theories without recognizing the differences between group as well as individual characteristics of the clients and those of Western cultures.

This chapter may serve as an eye-opener for both Muslim clients and counselors. For Muslims, it explains points of similarities as well as causes of diversity among various Muslim cultures. It also shows the influences of social, economic, political, and cultural factors on religious understanding and practice.

The diversity among American Muslims is the result of a combination of past experiences and present life situations as well as expectations and the future arena of actions. This means that values of American Muslims can be classified into four main categories:

(a) Universal values are what Muslims share with members of all other groups, particularly with religious ones and even more so with the two monotheistic religions, Judaism and Christianity. All humans share universal characteristics regardless of their race, color, or religion, while people of various religious affiliations have been found to have more in common than with non-religious communities. They share some beliefs and values. For instance, beliefs they share are the belief in God, prophets, scriptures, and life after death. The values include, although to varying degrees, charity as a social obligation, respect for human life, and yearning for justice and equality.

(b) The American experience including historical, social, economic, political, and cultural factors and influences make the American Muslim community share common values, aspirations, and opinions that are not necessarily shared by other world Muslim communities.

(c) Group commonality, which means that the values and norms of each Muslim subgroup are a combination of that group's experience of Islam in addition to its own intercultural settings.

(d) Individual characteristics, such as interests, activities, and traits. While acknowledging such individual characteristics, the influence of religion and culture on those individuals must not be ignored.

On the one hand, this means that American Muslims share universal values with the rest of humanity and also share elements of group commonality with other racial, ethnic, and national groups that are not Muslims. On the other hand, American Muslims may differ greatly from other world Muslim communities that share neither the experience nor the dreams of American Muslims.

To illustrate, African American Muslims share universal values with the rest of the world's Muslims, yet they are different from them in what constitutes their unique African American identity, historic, and cultural experience. Furthermore, individual factors among members of the same African American Muslim community account for individual differences within this particular group. Instead of applying the widespread dangerous assumption that "one size fits all," this complex makeup of identity needs to be acknowledged when dealing with American Muslims.

For counselors, this chapter provides the essential information for understanding their Muslim clients at a deeper level and consequently recognizing the complexity of their issues and concerns. Counselors must depart from the mid-twentieth-century tradition in which religious authorities tend to describe their religion on its most profound level while describing other religions on their most superficial levels, as "futile human attempts to reach God," as outlined by the theologian Paul Tillich (Miles, 1998). To that extent, Sundberg and Sue (1989) assert, "Intercultural counseling is enhanced by the knowledge of the client's degree of identification with the relevant cultures and the use of cultural reference group members who are most important in their lives" (p. 351).

The need for counselors to learn about different aspects of the Islamic faith and Muslim cultures is vitally important to making their interactions with their Muslim clients much more effective and productive. Such understanding cannot be assumed without serious efforts from counselors to examine sources of information and overcome widespread prejudices about Muslims. This will also help counselors identify the level of prejudice, misunderstanding, and consequently discrimination in society against the Muslim population, and this in turn may explain some of the anger and frustration that some Muslim clients may have toward society. Therefore, counselors are asked to learn more about their own assumptions and biases related to Muslims, thus allowing them to understand the real issues and concerns of their Muslim clients from their point of view.

This presents us with another dynamic in the formation of the perception and attitude of American Muslims. This dynamic is the constant struggle between the old and newly adopted cultures. Whether indigenous or immigrants, American Muslims may develop feelings of resentment and fear of the new culture (i.e., the American), thus leading them to adopt more conservative practices than the ones practiced at home or in other Muslim countries.

Counseling Muslims must, therefore, incorporate their ideological beliefs, cultural traditions, family support systems, and personal experiences. It must also include the cultural conflicts that may not be recognized by the clients themselves.

Most Muslims, regardless of their cultural or ethnic backgrounds, may have to face, at one time or another, difficult situations related to the lack of sensitivity to Islamic dietary restrictions. This could happen in homes with non-Muslim family members, in hospitals, in schools, and in other public facilities. Examples include young Muslim converts living in their parents' homes, Muslim children in school cafeterias, and Muslim patients in hospitals.

It is advisable that counselors keep handy in their offices some guides regarding Islamic rules and regulations related to these issues. At the same time, it would be helpful to keep a directory of local and national Islamic organizations that can help in the counseling process or in answering the counselor's questions.

Young Muslims may be dealing with issues that cause interruption to the long-held tradition of the family or to the religious practices of the group. Such issues include respect of parents in the traditional sense, relationships that are not approved by the family for either religious or cultural reasons, interracial and interreligious marriages, peer pressure, academic issues, and career counseling.

QUESTIONS FOR DISCUSSION

1. Where do the majority Muslim populations live?
2. What is the Islamic view of the world?
3. What do Muslims of diverse background have in common and what do they not share?
4. What are the tenets of Islam?
5. How did Muslims come to North America?
6. Are all Muslims the same? Why or why not?
7. How many major Muslim sects are there? What are the differentiating factors? What is the population size of each sect?
8. Provide a comparison of the status of Muslim women between that of Islam and that of Muslim societies.

9. How do counseling issues differ between immigrant, African American, and European American Muslims?

10. What are the different stages of development from the point of view of Muslims? How are they the same or different from those in Western cultures?

11. What are the unifying elements among American Muslims? What are the elements of diversity among them?

12. How are Muslims similar to and how are they different from the general population?

13. How does the degree of acculturation affect both the client and the counselor with respect to counseling?

14. What are the factors that affect Muslims seeking or going to a counselor?

CHAPTER 3

American Muslims and Their Perception of Psychotherapy

A stigma (i.e., negative perception) attached to seeing a counselor, a therapist, or other mental health professional is commonplace among members of various ethnic, professional, age, religious, and cultural groups (Bekkum, 1994; Deane & Chamberlain, 1994; Docherty, 1997; Langman, 1995; Misumi, 1993; Pugh et al., 1994; Szivos & Griffith, 1990; Schore, 1990). Going to counseling can be seen as a sign of failure (Schore, 1990). Among the most prevailing potential sources of counseling fears are fear of embarrassment, fear of change, fear of stereotypes linked to treatment, fears associated with past experiences with the mental health service system, and fears of negative judgment (Kushner & Sher, 1991, cited in Deane & Chamberlain, 1994).

Furthermore, the family, peers, work environments, and the mental health service institutions have been found to be very influential in the development of negative attitudes toward mental health services (Deane & Chamberlain, 1994; Docherty, 1997; Folkenberg, 1986; Juarez, 1985; Lefley, 1989; Root, 1985; Sundberg & Sue, 1989; Tanaka-Matsumi & Higginbotham, 1989).

This kind of stigma is regarded as one of the variables that causes individuals not to report their problems to primary care physicians for the fear of being referred to counseling, therapy, or other mental health professions. When counseling or therapy is imposed on them, clients demonstrate resistance more often than not by refusing to cooperate with therapists, thus limiting or inhibiting the professionals' ability to reach proper diagnosis, which is the first step toward effective treatment. According to Kushner and Sher (1991) and cited by Deane and Chamberlain

(1994), "Stigma has been identified as a key avoidance motive in help-seeking as well as a treatment barrier" (p. 208). Among other variables is the lack of awareness of the nature of the illness and its symptoms so that they can be reported accurately to physicians (Docherty, 1997).

In this chapter, I describe the ways in which American Muslims perceive counseling and therapy. This will help show a contrast between the perceptions and attitudes of American Muslims toward counseling and those of the general population.

Muslims' stigma regarding mental health professionals, procedures, facilities, and services may have been dynamically formed and enforced by culture, religion, or a combination of the two. Muslims' attitudes toward counseling are greatly affected by such stigma. As a result of this stigma, going to counseling is usually done, in most cases, at the insistence of some external authority, such as a parent, a spouse (particularly the husband), a family doctor, a court's judge, a superior, a teacher, or a school's principal.

I have to distinguish between formal and informal counseling. The information provided in this chapter reflects Muslims' responses to settings of formal counseling. Informal counseling occurs more frequently and in less formal settings. Counseling from imams (i.e., spiritual leaders), parents, teachers, and so on, for instance, occurs in an educational context rather than a medical model format. Informal counseling is not, however, the focus of this book. Muslim clients' response to and acceptance of informal counseling may be different than that to a counselor or a therapist even though they may be saying the same thing.

THE ROLE OF RELIGION IN MUSLIMS' PERCEPTION OF COUNSELING

Individuals' experiences are shaped by dynamics of cultures, religion, race, and ethnicity (Lee, 1991). Religion, being a source of identity and meaning, plays an important role in the construct of the individual's well-being. The consensus of researchers and writers is that the religiosity of clients must be evaluated and their religious values must be taken into consideration in order for the counselor to deliver effective counseling (Dwairy, 1998; Ibrahim, 1991; Jackson, 1991; Kelly, Aridi, & Bakhtiar, 1996; Lee, 1991). In particular, religious individuals of the Muslim community may see all issues as religious (Altareb, 1996). Among my clients, I found that culture and religion are often confused with each other, and, as is the case with most Muslims, there is no clear distinction between the two. According to Kelly et al. (1996), 86 percent of religious Muslim clients in their research said that it is very important for the counselor to know beforehand about their religion. In my interviews with subjects, I found that religion was not an issue in making the decision whether to seek counseling. Religion became an issue only after the counseling sessions began. To illustrate the lack of distinction between culture and religion, let us consider Pride, who is seeking full authority and control over her children, including the right to beat them. In justification of her position, she mentioned her family's history and her South Asian cultural experience as references to and sources for understanding her religious values. She said, "The culture—our Muslim rules—how children would behave with parents and the good things about Muslim—how do I say? The way we grew up in our country, in our Islamic way is different than here. So Americans only know about their culture."

It is obvious that Pride considers Islam and the way she grew up as one and the same. It is not uncommon to see Muslim individuals confusing cultural ways with religion. Such confusion affects the client's attitude toward counseling; it also creates barriers between Muslims on the basis of cultures, while they perceive such differences as religious. This phenomenon supports Geertz's (1973) description of religion as a "cultural system."

Hikmat believes that religion can be a factor only if the problem is of a religious nature. Deciding on the criteria of choosing a counselor, he states,

But in our case, the problem which we ran into—that was a creation of this culture, that is eating disorder. That's a problem which our kid acquired from this culture. So for that particular reason, since it came from this culture, anybody pretty much could handle that. But had it been a problem which had roots in our previous culture or religion. Then the people we went to for help, it would have been difficult.

Counselors need not be Muslims themselves in order to be able to display understanding of Islam, show sensitivity to Muslim clients and consequently earn their trust, and develop the rapport necessary for successful outcome. In fact, it is to the contrary. Clients expressed their preference for a counselor who is not a Muslim over one who is a Muslim. Among the reasons they cited was the concern over the breach of confidentiality.

For some religious groups, mental health deficiency may be seen as beyond another person's ability to help, and therefore a person seeks to resolve this issue by becoming closer to God or through traditional methods (Lee, Oh, & Mountcastle, 1992). This attitude is also common among many Muslims. The word *majnun*, used in Arabic to describe the mentally ill, means possessed by a demon, something beyond anyone's control. The most essential element in this regard is, therefore, the client's view of the nature of the problem. If the client perceives it as religion based or related, the counselor's approach must accommodate such a view. In cases where counselors dismiss the role of religion against the client's beliefs, the outcome proves unsuccessful. To illustrate, Farida was traumatized by the murder of her husband, who owned a grocery store in which he used to sell, in violation of Islamic principles, alcoholic beverages and pork. The indulgence of Farida's husband in these Islamically prohibited acts traumatized her even further. She feared that he might be suffering in hell. The counselor downplayed and even dismissed Farida's beliefs and fears, thus leading to the termination of the counseling relationship.

Religion for Muslims could impact social situations as broadly differentiated as grief, guilt, family relations, discrimination, dress code, and career issues. Drawing strength and support from religion could be more helpful to addressing clients' concerns than ignoring it. Such ability requires counselors to develop an understanding of both the clients' belief systems as well as their evaluations of the nature of their concerns.

THE ROLE OF CULTURE IN MUSLIMS' PERCEPTIONS OF COUNSELING

By culture, I mean the societal conditioning that influences the individual's perception of counseling as well as the decision whether to seek it. In this section, I use my clients' views supported by literature to develop an understanding of how Muslims view and respond to counseling.

It is important to note that not all Muslims have negative perceptions of counseling. In fact, some people may have no hesitation in going to counseling. Wahida, for instance, is a white American woman who is in her thirties. She converted to Islam when she was a teen, married a Middle Eastern man, and moved to live with him in his country, leading what she describes as "a very strict life both culturally and religiously." After living more than 10 years in that Middle Eastern country, she separated from her husband and returned to the United States to live with her children. When she thought she needed counseling, she did not have difficulty going to a counselor. Her attitude toward counseling and therapy is best illustrated by her following statement: "Well, I became frustrated and depressed, and so I needed counseling—obviously, growing in America, counseling is an 'in' thing for every one—you know therapy. During most of my teenage years, therapy was very popular. So when I came home and realized that I was going through all these stages here, I needed to get help. So that's what I had focused on—to go get therapy."

Wahida's exposure to counseling and therapy in the United States before marriage appears to have helped in the development of her positive attitude toward counseling and therapy. The years that she spent in that Middle Eastern country where seeking help outside the family is seen as invasion of the family's privacy did not change such an attitude. Clients' previous experiences with therapy are, therefore, very important in determining their future attitudes toward it.

Wahida's attitude toward counseling and therapy, however, is not common among members of the Muslim community, especially nonwhite

American Muslims. With respect to the negative perception of counseling and therapy among Muslims, the following cases represent the dominant views among the American Muslim community.

According to statistics, the majority of the American Muslim community in the United States is made up predominantly of nonwhites (i.e., African Americans and immigrants). While African Americans are considered underserved because of racism, the immigrant group can be described as having had little or no exposure to therapy as it is known in the United States today. From my clients' experiences, I found the following barriers to be strong and dominant among American Muslims, particularly those of immigrant backgrounds.

Equating Counseling with Mental Illness

Aslam is a Canadian Muslim immigrant who came originally from the Indian subcontinent. He has an undergraduate degree and works as a computer engineer in the United States. He suffered from symptoms of anxiety and obsessive-compulsive disorder, which threatened both his career and his marriage. In addition to the pain and suffering, all aspects of his life have been affected by his conditions. When I suggested further medical and psychological evaluation, he literally stopped seeing me for two months, during which I assumed that he must have begun the course of treatment with a specialist. When we unexpectedly met, he greeted me and waited until I was alone, then said, "I know you'll say I have a mental problem or crazy or something."

Many Muslims, like Aslam, equate personal developmental problems, career concerns, and mental health conditions with craziness and insanity. Those who do not do so fear the stigma attached to such services by Muslim peers, friends, or relatives.

Farida is an Arab American and a mother of three children, one of whom is handicapped. She struggled over whether she should go to therapy to help her cope with feelings of embarrassment that resulted in withdrawal from her relatives and the Arab community. She also needed to learn how to deal with her child's needs and enhance his development. Finally, she went to a therapist, only on the insistence of her doctor and social worker, but kept it a secret simply because she could not share with her friends and relatives that she was receiving psychotherapy. Farida explains,

This particular subject [therapy], I didn't talk to an Arabic person, or Muslim about it. I used to just talk to American people about it. Because Arabic people—they think we're crazy because we go to a counselor, but American People—they say, "it will help-you find someone to talk to." But Arabic people, they would think I'm not stable enough to handle life and to handle the stress that's why I go to therapy.

Seeking counseling can therefore be seen, as Farida stated, as a sign of weakness and possibly of insanity. In support of Farida's assumptions, Dwairy (1998) states, "Arabs tend to tolerate mental and emotional disturbances as long as they are not expressed in undue violence, shameful behavior, or uncontrollable overactivity. In general, they tend to pathologize abnormal behaviors. . . . Arabs do not seek help in psychotherapy. They do not believe that talking about problems helps. Also, referral to psychotherapy carries a stigma. Instead they seek help from physicians or traditional healers who apply anti-sorcery and anti-envy rituals" (p. 131).

Many Muslim communities around the world hold the same view of mental health professions as that of Arabs. As stated earlier, Pride, who comes originally from the Indian subcontinent and has been in the United States for more than 25 years, has displayed similar attitudes. She says,

I didn't know [about counseling] before. I knew about psychiatrists and I knew that people only go if they are mentally ill. At that time, I found out that counseling is not that you are mentally ill, but rather you have some problem and you want to discuss it.

Most Muslims are not any different. The daughter of the Hikmat family, for instance, is a college student who is American born and raised. She knew beyond a doubt that she was having eating-disorder problems. She went to a counselor with her friend who had a similar problem disguised as a supporter while, in fact, she was going mainly to discover for herself. She states, "When I was going to that counselor, I was just acting that I was there for my friend." Going with a friend might have helped her indirectly through undoing her long-held traditional perception of counseling.

For these reasons, counseling can be considered only the last resort for help. Furthermore, many Muslims worry about the way they are viewed by the rest of their communities, in which seeking counseling or treatment is equated with insanity.

Viewing Counseling as a Threat to One's Own Autonomy, Authority, or Status

A hierarchical family system among the majority of Muslims, where parents and elders receive the highest respect and enjoy unchallenged authority, has both religious and cultural foundations. Therefore, promoting individualism, equal rights, and democratic relations among family members, which are dominant values in American culture, threatens the willingness of many authority figures among American Muslim families to seek counseling. Furthermore, it will affect the effectiveness of such services when and if they are sought.

Karim, for instance, is an African American Muslim male who ada-mantly refused his wife's repeated appeals to join her in seeking coun-seling for the sake of saving their marriage, saying, "I am not going to go to another man to tell me what to do." Going to a woman counselor would have been considered even worse by Karim and like-minded Muslim males. When he finally made an appointment, he changed his mind and canceled the appointment at the last minute. Unfortunately, their marriage did not survive and was eventually terminated.

In addition, when counseling is perceived as a threat to the authority of parents in a parent–child relationship, counseling may never be sought voluntarily. Pride preferred going to a female counselor from outside the Muslim community because, as she put it, of two reasons: she feels more comfortable talking to a female counselor, something that is not available in the local Muslim community, and she feels that by going to a non-Muslim counselor, she will be at a lower risk of breaching confidentiality. Although she found a counselor who met her criteria, she quit counseling after only two sessions because of the fear of compromising her authority over her children. Pride states,

Like in our country we can scold the children—tell them not to do things. Here they have rules not to punish and not to hit the children. . . . In our country, the parents have authority over the children but here no, children come first. . . . The parents should not say certain things. We have to say things the proper way, give explanation. In our country we don't see that much. We say what is right and what is wrong. Children listen to the parents and do what the parents decide.

Although this statement is a gross generalization about American cul-ture and what parents can or cannot do with their children, Pride seems to be looking for unquestioned authority over her children. She does not want for her children to be able to even ask, let alone challenge parents' decisions, a cultural practice rather than a religious mandate of Islam. Men and elders commonly exert this strict control in many South Asian cul-tures over women and younger people. The idea behind restriction is to keep control and maintain order in the household and in society. In de-scribing this aspect of Karimpur culture, Wadley (1994) states, "Women should not be seen by strange men, nor should they talk to them. Un-married teenage girls are also restricted in their mobility, perhaps visiting the village shop for some spices or supplies for a festival, but always accompanied by other children" (p. 53).

It is obvious that the containment and control that parents exert on younger children are deeply rooted in cultural practices of various cul-tural groups.

When counseling children and families, Western psychotherapy com-monly attempts to establish a new set of rights and obligations for the parents and the children. A new family system is drawn to replace the existing one. It is customary for family therapists to treat each family member as equal and consequently treat their opinions and wishes with equal attention and respect (Foley, 1989; Haley, 1967; Minuchin, 1974). This approach may not be as effective with Muslim populations as it is with other populations or groups. To the contrary, it may even prove counter-productive and dangerous. Dwairy (1998) states, "This democratic approach, in which all family members are accepted and valued equally, is inherently threatening to the hierarchical structure of Arabic families. In this culture, all family members are not considered equal and respect is unidirectional toward the authority figure in the family. Attempts to impose these liberal attitudes will be met with strong resistance from the parents, especially the father" (p. 137).

In support of this point across various cultures, similar findings were reported with Arab American families (Abbudabbeh, 1996, pp. 333–346) Indonesian families (Piercy, Soekandar, & Limansuborto, 1996, pp. 316–323), Asian American families (Lee, 1996, pp. 227–248), Iranian families (Jalali, 1996, pp. 347–363), African American Muslim families (Mahmoud, 1996, pp. 112–128), Indian Muslim families (Almeida, 1996, pp. 395–426), and Nigerian families (Nwadiora, 1996, pp. 129–140).

Maintaining such a tradition of the parent–child relationship in the context of American culture represents a challenge to members of the Muslim community, as Jackson (1991) states:

Children are raised in a manner that ensures that they will respect their parents. In Arabic culture, good children show respect for their parents as well as for all adults, particularly older adults. Recently, however, many Arab American children have been rejecting their cultural traditions. Parents now have to spend more time and effort to exert control and instill traditional discipline in their children. Peer pressure in schools, for example, has begun to compete with parental influence. (p. 200)

This presents the field and professions of mental health with a greater challenge: how to strike a balance between personal, cultural, or religious interests of clients (in this case, parents and children) within the boundaries of the law and the Constitution.

My recommendations in this respect are to first help the client identify the origin of his or her beliefs about such practices. Consequently, the client's conviction of and insistence on such excessive control over the children will be lessened. As a comparison between the benefits and the possible harms of either case, allowing the children their reasonable rights versus suppressing them will clearly be helpful in identifying parents' faulty thinking about the effectiveness of outdated modes of discipline. Counselors must always maintain that they understand parents' concerns being for the good of the children. Unlike many Muslim cultural traditions, Islam allows children recourse when they are treated unfairly by parents. The Prophet of Islam issued judgments for children against their parents without breaking the relationship or the family.

Seeking Help May Be Seen as an Expression of Lacking Family, Friends, and Supportive Relatives

In a study on Arab Americans, Jackson (1991) states that "loyalty to one's family takes precedence over personal needs" (p. 199). This is also true for the various cultures within the Muslim community, particularly immigrants, who have always relied on their traditional support systems for solutions to their problems. When it comes to counseling, the first priority for a client is to seek help from a family member who may be a father or an elder member (Jackson, 1991). Counselors must not lose sight of the sensitivity of the relationship. While helping parents learn new ways of communicating with children and understanding their children's concerns, they must also stress keeping the children's respect for their parents despite disagreements.

Going to a counselor may be seen as a breech in family unity by, according to Farida, "having to pay a stranger to listen to you talk about a personal problem." Among most Muslims, this is considered weird and implies that "you have no friends or family that you rely on and that you can't handle things on your own," Farida says. In other words, seeking professional counseling is regarded in most Muslim cultures as the last resort when all other traditional sources of support and advice are not available or have not been helpful.

When asked where she would go for counseling had she been in her home country, Pride said, "We have parents; we have our grandparents we can talk with; we have a brother, a sister. . . . Let me tell you that in our country, we wouldn't go to a counselor that easily. Here we need the counselor, someone we can talk with. We have no family here so, we need the counselor to talk with."

During his counseling relationship with me, Aslam missed many sessions because of, as he stated, feelings of shame, embarrassment, and guilt for taking his private life outside the family to a stranger.

Labibah, a college student, sought counseling only on her parents' insistence after having avoided it for several months just for the fear of having to disclose her family's affairs, including her childhood, to a stranger. She describes herself as feeling "hesitant to seek counseling." She was not comfortable with strangers digging into her past and family issues. Not too long after seeing a counselor, she decided to quit because she "did not want to say anything bad about her parents to a stranger."

Counseling relationships can, therefore, be interrupted and possibly terminated when the client feels that loyalty to one's family members and family ties is at risk.

Lack of Knowledge and Awareness of the Existence, Procedures, and Expected Outcome of Counseling

Lack of awareness of the availability and expectations of counseling and psychotherapy professions hinders people's use of their services. Most Muslims either lack the information necessary to make informed decisions about counseling or learn such information from secondary and unreliable sources. Such information is usually neither complete nor accurate. I found knowledge and awareness of therapy to be strongly linked to the length of stay in the United States as well as to whether the person has received or is related to one who has received education in U.S. academic institutions.

Hikmat's wife, Halimah, is a mother of four children, two of whom have already graduated with doctoral degrees. Both the third and the fourth are in college. Halimah has been in the United States since the mid-1970s. Hikmat, who obtained his Ph.D. from a U.S. university, knew about the existence and availability of counseling since the time of his graduate studies. As a family, the Hikmats have never discussed the issue of counseling at home. Halimah remained unaware of the existence of counseling until her children began high school. This suggests that Muslim families, after learning of counseling, may think that it is not relevant to their lives and, therefore, should not be included in their discussions. Halimah states,

Well, I didn't know until my children were in high school, and in high school they do have counseling for children, and I found out from my daughter that they don't just have counseling for children, they even have it for parents. So that's how I got to know. I did not know before. I knew about psychiatrists. At that time, I found that counseling is not that you are mentally ill, but rather that you have some problem and you want to discuss it.

What happens inside counseling and psychotherapy sessions is also a mystery to most Muslims. Because of the strong desire for confidentiality on which most Muslims insist, the opportunity for discussing what goes on in counseling sessions between those who have been in counseling and potential clients is null or, at best, is kept to a minimum. To many, the main source of education on the profession is left to television, Hollywood movies, and fiction.

Labibah is an American-born college student who lives with her Asian American aristocratic family. She says that she did not know about counselors before going to high school. She got to know about them through her classmates who received help in guidance as well as in other issues.

When asked about her expectations as to what she thought would happen to her in counseling before she went for the first time, Labibah said, "Well, I expected a lot of questions and I expected the person to go to childhood and sort of just analyze everything—I mean, from TV and from movies and reading, [I expected] a lot of questions and them going into—trying to make connections to what the current situation is and what could be the reason in the past."

The accuracy of Labiba's assumptions about what goes on in counseling sessions may be questionable, but the undeniable fact is that, despite her awareness of the existence of counseling, her perception of it and of counselors intensified her unwillingness to seek help through it.

The use of a particular basic theory or technique depends very much on the counselor's personal preference, experience, and training. Since the client's benefit should be given a priority over the orientation of the counselor, the client's variables must be included as essential elements in the determination of education and training of counselors rather than leaving it to the counselor's convenience. What may be very helpful in this regard is to encourage counselors to adapt the theories and techniques that are more beneficial to their clients and not be encapsulated in a particular theory or model (Corey, 1991). For example, among various psychological theories and therapeutic approaches, psychoanalytic therapy is the one that is perceived as digging into the childhood of an individual. Basic to the foundation of this school is the belief that human beings are determined by early developmental experience. Personality problems are seen as caused by early developmental experiences that can be understood by unlocking repressed childhood conflicts (Corey, 1991). This approach may be seen as intrusive and offensive to reserved Muslims. Furthermore, this approach requires time and constitutes financial liability, both of which are beyond the abilities of clients with pressing needs, such as refugees whose situations are usually urgent and require immediate solutions.

The issues for which counseling can be sought are also unknown. Halimah states,

One other thing is that people need to know what counseling is and why you would go to counseling. People don't know. One of my friends—her daughter just got divorced. She was having problems with her in-laws. I said, "Well, why doesn't she go to counseling?" She said, "Why would she go to counseling? She wasn't having problems with her husband, she was having problem with her in-laws." I said, "That's what they will teach you—how to be with in-laws." But she would not understand. She said, "No, you go to a counselor if you have husband-wife problems; you don't go to counselors if you have in-law problems." I said, "No you should go."

There is no doubt that information on therapy communicated by former or current clients will be at best incomplete and will not take the mystery out of it. The field of mental health must, therefore, adequately publicize its services among minority groups, particularly the ones who are the least informed about it. This publicity must take various formats and utilize several media. It must also communicate information on the following elements:

(a) The functions of therapy and counseling
(b) The education and training of counselors and therapists, including multicultural education and training
(c) The scope of counseling and therapy, in other words, the issues for which counseling and therapy can be helpful
(d) The procedures which clients should expect during sessions
(e) The expected outcome of counseling
(f) The financial liability for clients

The dissemination of such information will help American Muslims seek counseling as soon as it becomes necessary or needed, and learn what issues to seek counseling for, how to choose a counselor, and what community resources, financial and otherwise, are available to them.

The Degree of Acculturation and Assimilation

Acculturation, within the context of American society, refers to the degree to which an individual identifies with the attitudes, lifestyles, and values of dominant macrocultures. For groups with non-European cultural origins, the development of ethnic identity has been conceptualized as an evolutionary stage process (Atkinson, Morten, & Sue, 1979; Cross, 1971; Jackson, 1975; Sue & Sue, 1971). Generally, these stages can range from strong identification with the macroculture to complete identification with the racial/ethnic group of origin. An individual's level of ethnic identity or acculturation may be influenced by a variety of factors, such as age, length of residence in the United States, level of education, extent of experience with racism, and socioeconomic status (Lee, 1991).

Among the clients in this study, the most common factors for seeking counseling were, after the exhaustion of all traditional means, the pressing need for counseling and the insistence of a significant family member.

The Hikmat family went to counseling only after their older daughter collapsed two times because of weakness that resulted from an eating disorder (anorexia nervosa) that frightened the whole family. Hikmat describes the situation by saying,

Since she was having problems and we were having communication problems with her, we almost started blaming each other—who did what which brought her to that point. So that was actually affecting our own relationship and we started drifting from each other and blaming each other. So that was the time that we felt that we actually needed counseling to really sort it out before it is too late.

Regardless of the history or beliefs that are behind anorexia nervosa, it is but a result of the popular culture that promotes certain body images as ideal to which everyone, especially females, must measure up. Brumberg (1989) states,

According to the cultural model, these class-specific ideas about body preference pervade the larger society and do enormous harm. The modern visual media (television, films, video, magazines, and particularly advertising) fuel the preoccupation with female thinness and serve as primary stimulus for anorexia nervosa. Female socialization, in the hands of the modern media, emphasizes external qualities ("good looks") above all else. As a consequence, we see few women of real girth on television or in the movies who also have vigor, intelligence, or sex appeal. Young girls, fed on this ideological pablum, learn to be decorative, passive, powerless, and ambivalent about being female. Herein lies the cause of anorexia nervosa, according to the cultural model. (p. 33)

Labibah was compelled to go to counseling by her parents because she was not doing well emotionally in school and expressed a desire to quit education altogether. In the case of Pride, she was forced to go to counseling despite her opposition to it when it became the only available alternative to divorce. In the case of Farida, she went to counseling because of her handicapped son, who caused her significant stress and, as she describes, embarrassment.

From my clients' responses, I found that education, particularly graduate and postgraduate, played a major role in advancing the process of acculturation, which, in turn, encouraged clients to seek counseling.

The husbands of both Pride and Halimah, for instance, received graduate degrees from American universities. Both men were the driving force for their wives to go to counseling. Although Pride quit counseling despite her husband's appeals, Hikmat, along with his family, stayed in counseling even after changing counselors. After going to the second counselor, they reported positive feelings toward counseling and the counselor. They also expressed satisfaction at the end of the counseling relationship that all their counseling goals had been met. Furthermore, they declared that they would not hesitate to go again to counseling if needed and that they would recommend it to anyone who encounters a problem.

Long residence in the United States without education, as in the case of Pride, or with partial undergraduate education, as in the case of Labibah, had no significant effect in changing clients' negative attitudes toward as well as concerns for the stigma of counseling and therapy. Hope for developing a positive attitude toward counseling may be totally diminished if the first client–counselor encounter does not provide clients with positive impressions. In fact, in the cases of both Pride and Labibah, the counseling relationship was terminated prematurely, and both subjects reported negative feelings and institutionalized fear of counseling after the first session and stated that the second and third sessions were not of additional help.

After going into counseling, the most important factors in the continuation of therapy seem to be the client's first impression of the counselor, feelings regarding the counselor, and the positive expectation of the counseling relationship. First impressions, often referred to as initial perceptions, have been found to be tenacious in interpersonal encounters (Marshall & Kratz, 1988). They have been found in counseling research to remain stable over time and to affect the process and outcome of psychotherapy (Cantor & Mischel, 1979; Tylor, Fiske, Etcott, & Ruderman, 1978).

Suspicion about the Counselor's Values and Feelings

Every culture has traditionally provided ways of dealing with psychological distress and behavioral deviance. For example, for the past century in the United States, counseling has evolved into a formal profession designed to help individuals resolve both situational and developmental problems in various aspects of their lives (Lee et al., 1992). Most American Muslims, however, are originally immigrants (approximately 55 percent of the total Muslim population in the United States) who come from mostly Eastern cultures and backgrounds. To this group of Muslims, counseling in the Western sense may be seen as a departure from the traditional culture that provides strength in dealing with issues of concern within the family and religion.

According to Lee et al. (1992), "Even though American mental health practices are becoming accepted in countries included in their study, indigenous treatment methods and procedures are extremely important and widespread. In most instances, these indigenous methods for treating psychological distress and behavioral deviance are centuries old. Two indigenous models of helping seem to be pervasive: kinship system and spiritualism-religion" (p. 5).

Most American Muslims neither want to perceive themselves nor want to be perceived by others as having abandoned their cultural heritage or their religion.

The largest ethnic group among the Muslim population is African American Muslims (approximately 43 percent of the total Muslim population in the United States). Mahmoud (1996) describes their attitude toward psychotherapy by saying,

There is a great deal of suspiciousness of Euro American therapists among the African American Muslim communities, both cultural nationalists and Sunni. It is rare for members to go outside of their community for advice or guidance. This suspiciousness I believe has grown out of the acute awareness of oppression brought about by intense study of African American history by many members, the historical reality of how Islam became associated with cultural nationalism, and the individual experiences of the members with racism which may have contributed to their conversion. The presence of prejudicial articles, media attention, and books that foster fear and dislike of Muslims and do little to educate the public about the religion as it is practiced by different groups is a main factor of such suspiciousness. (p. 124)

The attitude of immigrant Muslims is also influenced by different yet similar social and political experiences as discussed in the previous chapter. Beginning with self-perception, images projected by the media and American foreign policies toward the Muslim and Arab worlds influence how Muslims develop perceptions of how others would treat them

American Muslims may, therefore, feel that counselors are also biased and that such biases will influence counselors' attitudes toward them. In addition, since all Muslims of the world are bound together as a community of faith (Al-Ahsan, 1992; Al-Faruqi, 1984; Altareb, 1996, 1997; Esposito, 1995), negative portrayal of foreign Muslims outside the United States will affect both Muslims and non-Muslims living in America. While it affects American non-Muslim's perceptions of Islam and Muslims, it also affects Muslims' perception of themselves and of American society and consequently leads to withdrawal and more isolation (Altareb, 1997; Haddad, 1998).

Delaying or ignoring therapy despite the need for it, among clients represented in this book, led in turn to the delay of desired outcomes that have been achieved as a result of counseling, as is the case with Hikmat's family and Farida. In Hikmat's case, the family was able to develop better relations and better understanding among each other, and their daughter was able to recover from the eating-disorder problem. Farida learned more ways to deal with her handicapped son, developed the courage not to shy away because of her son's disability, became aware of community resources, and joined support groups.

Muslims' fear seems to stem from existing value differences. From clients as well as from the literature, the following values have been commonly found among the Muslim population:

- A person's dignity, honor, and reputation is of paramount importance.
- Loyalty to one's family takes precedence over personal needs.
- It is important to behave at all times in a manner that reflects well on others.
- Everyone believes in one God and acknowledges His power.
- Humans cannot control all events; all things depend on God.
- Piety is among the most admirable characteristics in a person. (Badri, 1979; Dwairy, 1998; Haddad & Lummis, 1987; Jackson, 1991; Jafari, 1993)

To conclude, in order for the counselors to enhance their effectiveness, they need to understand the values and beliefs of their clients, be sensitive in dealing with them, and assure their clients of respect and accommodation.

DISCUSSION AND IMPLICATIONS FOR COUNSELING

Counseling is almost unknown to Muslims. It is, therefore, very important for professionals, associations, and service-providing agencies to widely publicize their services among the Muslim population. Such publicity will help Muslim clients realize the potential benefits counseling can provide for them.

For Muslims who know of counseling from secondary sources, they see it, more likely than not, as negative and undesirable. Such negative attitudes and perceptions of Muslims toward counseling have both religious and cultural bases.

To help in dealing with religiously based negative perceptions toward counseling, professionals need to collaborate with officials of Islamic local and national organizations in conducting seminars aimed at addressing Muslim communities and answering their questions about various issues related to counseling and therapy. By explaining counseling and assuring respect for the religious as well as cultural backgrounds of their clients, counselors would encourage Muslim clients to seek counseling. Furthermore, identifying the issues for which counseling and therapy can be sought will help Muslim clients act as soon as they are faced with such issues.

Muslim leaders can help by citing several Islamic religious textual statements that encourage seeking benefits and treatments as long as they are not in direct conflict with Islamic principles.

Teaming up with Muslim physicians in the region of the therapist would also help in providing Muslim clients with confidence, since referrals to therapy and counseling are often made by clients' Muslim physicians.

These joint efforts can also help in issues where religion is confused with cultures by clients. It will also raise the awareness needed to present counseling as a possible alternative to traditional support systems that may not be available to them in the United States or may not fully meet their needs for variety of reasons, including economic ones.

Therapists also need to counsel clients from the clients' own perspectives and not from their own. While it is required of them to champion the causes of their clients to implement justice and end discrimination, they should not at any time expose the client to a risk that the client is not ready for or willing to undertake.

Traditional means of counseling that have been utilized for a long time must also be examined and encouraged if proven to be helpful. Counselors can be of great help if they display sensitivity and respect and if they assure their clients of the confidentiality of their participation in counseling and of the issues they present. Clients with issues concerning family relations, for instance, will not seek counseling if the counselors operate with a bias toward what may be perceived as individualistic and materialistic values. For Muslim clients, this may be seen as taking family members farther apart from each other instead of bringing them closer. Furthermore, the employment of psychoanalytical approaches with Muslim families may delay or hinder the cultural adjustment that is urgently needed, further mistrust in counseling when family relations are examined, or prove costly and unaffordable in case of low-income families (e.g., refugees).

Because Muslim clients tend to tolerate psychological distress and describe their emotional problems in somatic terms, it is important for counselors to understand their clients' perceptions of mental health as well as of therapy. In terms of the counselor–client relationship, resistance, denial, and skepticism of counseling and counselors will create a need for more time to develop a positive relationship between the counselor and the Muslim client (Mahmoud, 1996). Dealing early with negative perceptions will help pave the way for the client's cooperation in dealing with issues of concern.

Clients who continue counseling are generally those who developed positive impressions from initial encounters. It is essential, therefore, for counselors to work on developing a rapport with their clients as early as the first session.

Since affordability is a concern to many people, including middle-class members of the Muslim community, particularly when the length of the counseling relationship is not known, counselors should use the shortest possible approach that can deal effectively with the client and with the concerns they present. Another way to combat high costs is to petition insurance companies and lobby the legislative branch to widen insurance coverage for counseling and psychotherapy. After all, healthier individuals and families contribute greatly to the well-being of society at large. Helping a client find suitable employment in the case of career counseling contributes to the economy of the entire country. The government uses taxpayers' money to pay for lawyers' services that they offer to suspected criminals. Couldn't the government, then, provide culturally competent counselors or therapists to those who are in need in order to remain functioning in society? This assistance will be repaid in the form of contributions that these individuals will be making to society when their lives are greatly improved.

It is obvious that because of discrimination against Muslims in schools, workplaces, and public spaces and because of U.S. foreign policies and practices, Muslims have developed what can be called a love–hate relationship with American society and culture. On the one hand, they love the opportunities of thinking freely and positive employment, which open the doors for all the affluence and achievements that America offers; on the other hand, they hate much of the prevailing American lifestyle and think of it as permissive, promiscuous, and even hedonistic. To Muslim clients, society's attitudes and practices, including counseling, may be seen as pandering to pleasure-seeking and pleasure-indulging personalities. Related to this conflict is the conflict between two cultures, in which the client has allegiance to more than one culture at once, that is, his or her culture of origin where he or she grew up and the second one where he or she enjoys living. In order for counselors to help Muslim clients reconcile the two views, counselors must be able to respect the client's views of both cultures instead of being judgmental about one or the other, and then productively explore the conflict during the counseling sessions.

CHAPTER 4

Counseling and Counselors

ORIGIN, SOURCES, AND DOMINATING FACTORS IN COUNSELING

I derive information in this chapter from interviews with two counselors, from the literature, and from my own study and experience to outline inherent values and dominant practices in counseling as we know it today and how they affect Muslim clients.

By doing this, I attempt to serve a dual purpose: to help counselors see how the counseling profession can become a tool of oppression because of the lack of competency in education, training, and sensitivity to Muslim clients, and to help Muslim clients formulate more realistic expectations, thus enabling them to overcome fears resulting from risk perception with respect to counseling. By *risk perception,* I mean the psychological conditioning that results in the unnecessary and unreal assumption of conflict between counseling services with the principles of the Islamic religion or with values and practices of the client's particular culture and subculture.

This chapter is organized into three parts:

Counseling: In this part, I outline the foundations and the inherent value system of counseling that may influence counselors' attitudes and relationships with their Muslim clients. It is worth noting that the reference made here is to formal counseling, which establishes itself with formal procedures and is occurring in formal contexts. These contexts require that professionals and practitioners, namely, counselors and therapists, be formally educated, trained, and licensed to practice.

Counselors: From interviews with two counselors, I explore the deficiencies in the educational as well as the training programs of counseling with respect to dealing with minority groups in general and with respect to the Muslim population in particular. Using one of the most widely accepted models for multicultural competencies, I point out how counselors can benefit from this model in helping their Muslim clients. Furthermore, I show how deficient this model is and how it can be improved.

Clients: Through the experiences of my clients as well as from firsthand experience, I use, as a case study, the ordeal of a Muslim family who has been victimized by both counselors and the institutions to which they belong. Furthermore, I illustrate the devastating effects of commonly used testing methods, evaluation techniques, and counseling approaches to Muslim clients.

Counseling

While everyone seems to understand counseling, it is apparent that different people understand it in many different ways. Narrowly defined, formal counseling is an applied social science with an interdisciplinary foundation that includes, among other things, psychology, sociology, cultural anthropology, education, economics, and philosophy (Glanz, 1974). According to Hansen, Stevic, and Warner (1982),

Each of these disciplines has made and continues to make its own contribution to counseling. From psychology, we learn about human growth and development; sociology provides insight into social structures and institutions; anthropology helps us understand the importance of culture. (p. 8)

The United States today comprises the most impressive combination of global, ethnic, and racial diversity in human history. Although the national origin of the population is so diverse, the dominant culture in the United States has been narrowly Eurocentric and often Anglocentric (Mazrui, 1991). The scholarly disciplines in the humanities and social sciences (particularly psychology) are all initially products of Western experience and thought (Sharabi, 1990). Draguns (1989) states, "Counseling is the product of twentieth-century Euroamerican civilization. In particular, its ethos is bound up with certain key features of American culture: individualism, egalitarianism, glorification of social mobility and social change. From the start counseling has been imbued with a strong sense of self-determination" (p. 5).

Many of the basic assumptions of counseling and therapy reflect the social, economic, and political context of the Western Euro-American cultures in which they developed. These dominant cultural assumptions are universally acceptable (Pedersen, Fukuyama, & Heath, 1989).

Jafari (1993) states, "Counseling has established itself as a helping profession with an academic base. Its establishment has been influenced largely by the socioeconomic, occupational, and technical changes found in western society" (p. 326).

The purpose of counseling is to provide for the individual's optimum development and well-being, but the individual functions in a social context, not in isolation. If counselors are to enhance the well-being of the individual, they must understand as many of the factors as they can that affect people; they must adopt an interdisciplinary approach. Such an approach is the product of our past and of the current demands made by the public we serve (Hansen et al., 1982). It should not be surprising to anyone that negative perceptions and attitudes toward Islam and Muslims prevalent in this culture must have dramatic effects on counselors' perceptions and attitudes when dealing with this population.

What Is Good Counseling?

Good counseling depends on factors related to (a) the counselors and how they see themselves, other people, and the world; (b) the clients, their perception of self and of the counselor, and their understanding of the objectives of counseling and their commitment to change and improvement; and (c) the counselor–client relationship. The quality of the client–counselor relationship ranks first among factors that facilitate growth in both parties in the relationship (Corey, 1991). This is because in the counselor–client relationship, counselors can prove their positive regards for their clients, their understanding of the nature of their clients' concerns, and their ability to be of help to their clients.

Focusing on the counselor for a moment, we find distinction between effective and ineffective helpers. What appears to make the difference is what helpers believe about empathy, self, human nature, and their own purposes. Effective counselors are concerned primarily with how the world appears from the vantage point of their clients. They hold positive beliefs about people, a positive view of themselves, and a confidence in their abilities (Combs, 1986; Corey, 1991).

Value-Free Counseling: Does It Exist?

For quite some time, the popular view was that therapists and counselors should and/or could be neutral with respect to their values. In an effort to make counseling value neutral, counselors were urged not to impose their values on their clients. The agreement of theorists is that values must not be imposed by the counselors. In reality, this has not been the case, as research findings have concluded that it is neither possible nor desirable for counselors to be neutral. In reality, the notion of neutrality is challenged by several factors.

First, counseling strategies and interventions are value based. Corey (1991) states, "The interventions they make as counselors are based on their values" (p. 12). Values are an inevitable and pervasive part of psychology and counseling that affect the direction and outcome of the counseling process. The counselor, therefore, influences the value system of the individual being counseled in many explicit and implied ways. Research findings available on the impact of values indicate that clients who improve the most during therapy are those who revise their values in the direction of those of the counselor, while the values of the unimproved client become less like those of the therapist (Rosenthal, 1955). Williamson (1965) also asserts that counseling cannot be valueless. Practically speaking, it is unrealistic and rather impossible to expect that values, knowingly or unknowingly, will not play a major role in the counseling process (Sprinthall, 1971).

The Western value system has a profound impact on counseling approaches, techniques, and processes, for it reinforces what is considered good according to the prevalent social standards, values, and norms. Counselors have been urged to acquire a true understanding of society. The quest for identity on the part of the client is in reality a search for meaning and significance, which is always value laden. The counselor's values are expressed in the form of desired behavioral outcomes of the therapeutic process (Jafari, 1993).

Second, the employment of values in the counseling process is inevitable. Among other things, one recent national survey revealed a consensus among a representative group of mental health professionals that certain basic values are important for healthy lifestyles and for guiding and evaluating psychotherapy (Jensen & Bergin, 1988). The following 10 values were thought by professionals to contribute to a positive, mentally healthy lifestyle: (a) a competent perception and expression of feelings; (b) a sense of being a free and responsible agent; (c) management of stress; (d) self-awareness and growth; (e) commitment to marriage, family, and other relationships; (f) self-maintenance and physical fitness; (g) having orienting goals and meaningful purpose; (h) forgiveness; (i) regulated sexual fulfillment; and (j) spirituality/religiosity.

Third, neutrality of counselors is neither possible nor healthy. The recommendation of experts and professionals is that it is neither possible nor desirable for counselors to be neutral with respect to values in the counseling relationship (Corey, 1991). Patterson (1989) and Corey (1991) contend that while it is inappropriate for a therapist to attempt to indoctrinate clients or to inculcate a system of values in them, it is not inappropriate for them to discuss their values openly with their clients. I argue that it may be inappropriate at times for counselors to discuss their values with their Muslim clients, particularly if the values appear judgmental or antagonistic or unrelated to the theraputic relationship.

Racism: How Values Influence Counseling

According to Ridely (1995), racism affects minority clients in the following ways:

- Minority clients are more frequently misdiagnosed than others.
- Minority clients are treated by less experienced or inexperienced professionals.
- Minority client are subjected to low-cost and low-quality care with the tendency to use medication more than with other clients.
- Minority clients are admitted to public institutions more than they are to private ones.
- Minority clients are either terminated prematurely or confined for a longer time than other clients.
- Minority clients report dissatisfaction with services more than other clients.

Draguns (1989) and Lorion and Parron (1985) have reached similar conclusions.

Is Religion a Factor in Counseling?

Only in recent years has there been an increased recognition of the need for counselors to consider the role of spiritual and religious issues in the lives of their clients, particularly racial and ethnic minority clients (Constantine, 1999). In 1961 three Catholic interest groups: the Catholic Counselors in APGA, the founders of the Catholic Counselor, and the National Conference of Guidance Counselors merged to become the National Catholic Guidance Conference (NCGC). It was not until 1977 that the NCGC became the Association for Religious and Value Issues in Counseling (ARVIC) (Miller, 1999). In the mid-1980s, ARVIC leaders realized that the term "religious" in its title was not encompassing enough, so there was discussion at the national board and state membership levels about adding the word "spiritual." In 1993, ARVIS changed its name to the Association for Spiritual, Ethical, and Religious Values in Counseling (Miller, 1999). Lee (1991) states, "Although religion is accepted as a major influence on human development, it is not always considered an important or appropriate aspect for the counseling process. However, multicultural counseling may be enhanced if the influence of religion or spirituality is considered a crucial dynamic in the helping process" (p. 15).

To illustrate the importance of religion and spirituality in counseling, the following nine competencies have been selected for review by the Counsel for Accreditation of Counseling and Related Educational Programs (CACREP) for the purpose of incorporating them into their revised standards.

According to Burke (1998)

In order to be competent to help clients address the spiritual dimension of their lives, a counselor needs to be able to: 1) explain the relationship between religion and spirituality, including similarities and differences, 2) describe religious and spiritual beliefs and practices in a particular context, 3) engage in self-exploration of his/her religious and/or spiritual beliefs in order to increase sensitivity, understanding and acceptance of his/her belief system, 4) describe one's religious and/or spiritual belief system and explain various models of religious/spiritual development across the life span, 5) demonstrate sensitivity to and acceptance of a variety of religious and/or spiritual expressions in the client's communication, 6) identify the limits of one's understanding of a client's spiritual expression, and demonstrate appropriate referral skills and general possible referral sources, 7) assess the relevance of the spiritual domains in the client's therapeutic issue, 8) be sensitive to and respectful of the spiritual themes in the counseling process as befits each client's expressed preference, and 9) use a client's spiritual beliefs in the pursuit of the client's therapeutic goals as befits the client's expressed preference. (p. 2, cited in Miller, 1999, p. 500)

Religion in the Counseling of Muslims

Because Islam presents itself as a total way of life, most Muslims may perceive every issue as religious. In their survey of a sample of Muslims, Kelly, Aridi, and Bakhtiar (1996) found that "Muslims in this sample were as a group quite religious, with almost half favoring strict Islamic observance and another third moderate observance. Over three quarters of the sample considered themselves to be quite religious. They were not, however, a homogenous group by any means, as shown by divided opinion on adherence to Islamic schools of law, sympathy to Sufism, and the relationship of human freedom and divine determination" (p. 216).

Whether religion is an integral part of a Muslim client's presenting issue depends, therefore, on the individual and the issue. For example, clients who identify strongly with being Muslims may feel as though all concerns are potentially religious issues. These individuals may be less likely to seek therapeutic services because they want their concerns addressed from an Islamic viewpoint (Kelly et al., 1996). Those who do not identify as strongly with their religion may not feel the same way.

Kelly et al. (1996) conclude,

The pattern of universal and mental health value differences between those favoring strict and moderate or adjusted Islamic observance and between the quiet and somewhat personally religious lead us to speculate that those Muslims who are more moderate or flexible in Islamic observance are more likely to include a secular dimension in their value orientation than strict-observance Muslims. (p. 16)

They also caution that the willingness of some respondents to add a secular dimension to their lives should be interpreted not as a nonreligious attitude but as a form of religiousness that considers a secular dimension a legitimate part of one's religious belief and practice (p. 216). What people do, then, is translated within an American context into a different understanding of Islamic practice (Altareb, 1996).

This can be best illustrated by Farida, whose husband was murdered while working in the grocery store that he owned. A counselor to help Farida was appointed by the Victim Witness Advocate Assistance program sponsored by the district attorney's office. During my first encounter with the client, I noticed that she was evasive and expressing feelings of shame that her husband used to sell alcoholic beverages and pork, which are clearly forbidden by Islamic law. While the shame may be related to her confession with a Muslim counselor, she has been suffering a great deal of guilt for not having stopped him from these practices before he died, something she felt will cause him to suffer in hell. Farida also complained of feeling guilty because she was not the ideal wife she would have been had she known that her husband was going to die soon. Farida describes,

Big guilt—I didn't know he was going to die that soon. I would have changed things; I wouldn't say no if he asked me for something. I wouldn't fight with him. There are so many things I would have done different. I would have been the best woman I could be to satisfy his needs and give him things he wants and cook what he wants and clean and just do whatever he wanted.

Farida's deeply felt grief and sorrow were met with a superficial treatment from the therapist who dismissed them as personal, temporary, and baseless emotions. In Arabic culture, the wife is required to please the husband even at the expense of her own pleasure. In traditional Islamic schools of thought, too, the woman is supposed to be obedient to her husband in matters that do not constitute a violation of Islam itself. So the client felt guilty for her failure to have been the ideal wife according to both religious and cultural norms. The therapist's response was described by Farida in the following statement: "He told me to look through the window and see the birds singing and flying from tree to tree. That should bring joy to your life. Look at your kids. Whether you feel guilty or not, it's not going to change your life. You have to deal with issues differently than you used to."

In fact, the therapist's comments about having "to deal with issues differently" may have intensified her anxiety and fear by reminding Farida of her new loneliness and that she has to face life as a soloist from now on.

In Arab, as well as in most Muslim cultures, the man (a husband, a father, or an elder brother) is the breadwinner of the family. Farida's husband did not leave any assets for her and their children. The store that he owned was immersed in large debts. She became, therefore, overwhelmed with the burden of having to support herself and her children financially while, at the same time, continuously caring for the disabled child without a break. She is also young, in her early thirties, and may be looking for marriage sooner or later. The fact that she has three children, one of whom is disabled, may be an obstacle to finding a suitable mate. In Arab cultures, a woman who marries after the death of her husband may be viewed as disloyal and uncaring. She may be isolated and looked down on. All these issues needed a knowledgeable, skilled, and sensitive counselor.

Biased Diagnosis and Treatment

As previously mentioned, typical racism affects minority clients in diagnosis, staff assignment, treatment modality, utilization, treatment duration, and attitudes (Draguns, 1989; Lorion & Parron, 1985; Ridely, 1995). The case study that can best illustrate the devastating effects of biased diagnosis is that of the Abed family. The Abeds are Palestinian Americans who migrated to the United States more than 15 years ago as a result of the Arab–Israeli conflict. The Abeds are known among their community to be reserved and deeply rooted in the Arab–Palestinian cultures and traditions. They are also known to be quietly religious. The father is a businessman, while the mother is a housewife. Amal and Marwah, 13 and 14 years old, respectively, are sisters among five other siblings. Although these two girls were born in the United States, they still maintain very strict cultural practices on their parents' instructions. The two girls go to a suburban middle school where most of the student population is white middle class. An older brother goes to the high school in the same school district.

As it appears from the family's history, there are political, cultural, and religious issues that influence the family's attitudes and practices in life. As is customary in the Arab tradition, communication between the sexes is kept to a minimum. The girls were not communicating at school, particularly with the male teachers and students. The school's counselor, also a male, after testing the two girls, labeled both of them speech impaired and committed them to speech therapy.

The school's only counselor, who counseled these two girls, had his hands full. In a very busy and highly populated school district, he was covering four schools alone, making misdiagnosis due to lack of thoroughness no surprise to anyone. Ms. Field, the intern counselor in the same school and one of the counselors interviewed for this study, described the school's counselor as a young, inexperienced man. Furthermore, being in a school with few minority students would make his cross-cultural experience at best very limited. Not seeking help from outside resources makes the case fit into a typical profile of racism in dealing with minorities. In such a profile, minority clients receive minimal contact, medication only, or custodial care rather than intensive psychotherapy.

When I asked the family (in Arabic) about how they feel about the counselor's diagnosis, the family dismissed it as false and unfounded. They also felt that the school's administration, counselors, and staff were "ganging up against them" just because they are Arabs and because they are Muslims. They also felt that the way in which the school communicated to them the need for counseling was inappropriate and insulting. They described the school's invitation to participate in counseling as threatening and similar to a court's summoning. They explained the girls' lack of participation, which has led to their labeling as "disabled," as a family-based issue. It became clear that the family had instructed the two girls not to communicate verbally or otherwise with males. Unfortunately, the therapist was a male. What made the situation even worse was that each girl was required to sit alone with the therapist behind closed doors, which was extremely frightening for them and for their family. They thought that the only way to stop these sessions for the girls was by not communicating with the speech therapist at all. Of great concern to the family was the label "disability." They feared that it may stigmatize the two girls for the rest of their lives, thus significantly limiting their marriage opportunities, the ultimate goal for girls in most Arab traditions and societies.

Furthermore, most Arab cultures tolerate, as previously stated, pain, mental or physical, as long as it does not lead to a violent behavior (Dwairy, 1998). Consequently, this particular family felt that American culture is "overpsychologized" and could be spoiling the children's ability to tolerate difficulties and hardships, a necessary preparation for adulthood responsibilities.

Cultural Bias in Testing and Assessment

One definition, among many, of assessment is that it "is a process of understanding and helping people cope with problems. In this process, tests are frequently used to collect meaningful information about the person and his or her environment" (Walsh & Betz, 1990, p. 12). Psychological assessment, therefore, includes four major parts: the problem, information gathering, understanding the information, and coping with the problem. In the stage of understanding the information, the process must involve an attempt to organize, interpret, and understand the person–environment relation within a theoretical perspective drawn from one of the many theories of personality and human development. Consequently, one must realize that people and environments are in constant transaction and that any assessment of the person is incomplete without some assessment of the environment. Walsh and Betz (1990) state, "We can't take the person out of personality; but at the same time, we cannot ignore the fact that environments, like people, have personalities and influence behavior" (p. 15).

Psychological assessment has been the subject of criticism for racial and cultural biases. In the United States, psychological assessments as well as the educational organizations are obsessed with quantitative data collection (Bogdan & Biklen, 1992; Walsh & Betz, 1990). As such, they are deficient from a qualitative perspective; quantified results, therefore, should be studied in context from a qualitative perspective (Bogdan & Biklen, 1992). Standardized aptitude and intelligence tests, for example, are generally tests that discriminate against minority groups through cultural bias. Cultural bias in tests manifests in one of three ways: content bias, bias in internal structure, and selection bias (Walsh & Betz, 1990).

In content bias, the test questions may be more familiar to one group than to another. Most tests have been declared biased in favor of white middle-class American males. Others suffer as a result. This would include minority groups, such as blacks, women, Hispanics, and other socioeconomic or racial groups. Arabs and Muslims are definitely of these groups. In fact, Arab Americans who are Muslims are the least accepted among other Arab immigrant groups by American society (Jackson, 1991).

According to Walsh and Betz (1990), "Most tests should be developed by panels of experts that includes the representation of women, Hispanics, and blacks, and members of lower socioeconomic status groups. These panel members both contribute to and evaluate the item pool with the objective of minimizing gender, race, cultural and class bias" (p. 413).

To my knowledge, no experts from either the Arab or the Muslim community have been invited to participate in the development of assessment tools that are not biased to Arab and Muslim clients. Psychological testing is used on children as well as on adults without the realization that it may do more harm than good. In the case mentioned here, there is no indication that the speech therapist has ever sought modification of the testing to accommodate the cultural and religious differences that affect the girls' behavior and attitude toward school and society in general.

Bias in internal structure means that the tests do not measure the same things in different clients. Tests, therefore, are not supposed to be used for the same purposes in different groups unless they are measuring the same construct as well. According to Walsh and Betz (1990), "Research comparing tests' internal structural characteristics across groups is needed" (p. 413). Since such tests have not been examined in relation to Arabs or Muslims, the test's results in the case study that resulted in labeling the girls disabled are rendered invalid.

Selection bias occurs when a test has different predictive validity across groups, a prime example being SAT scores, which may have more predictive validity with the white middle-class population than with any other groups.

Biases in tests and assessments in psychology, be they in content, internal structure, or selection, have adverse impacts on minority groups in education, hiring, diagnosis, and treatment.

Counselors

Both counselors I interviewed represent indicative trends in the education, training, and understanding of issues related to Muslims and consequently the treatment they provide to their Muslim clients. They represent two different generations. Mr. Jones is in his late forties with almost 12 years of experience, while Ms. Field is in her late twenties, doing her internship before graduation from the master's program.

From my interviews with both counselors, I discovered some patterns that could be indicative of a culture or at least a condition. Prior to their experience with Muslim clients, both counselors did not consider the presence of Muslims in the clientele population, let alone the need for knowledge and training on how to deal with them. When facing Muslim clients, both counselors thought that they were capable of dealing with their clients without outside help, nor did they seek any outside help in dealing with their Muslim clients, except in the case of Ms. Field, but only when she reached a crisis in her counseling relationship. Yet another pattern was the institution's refusal to let their counselors seek training or support from the outside in order to enhance their ability to deal with Muslim clients. Ms. Field had to literally struggle against the school's administration in order to bring an outsider in to help improve the service to the Muslim children involved. The reason cited for such resistance was not in any way a concern for the children or the family but rather an insistance on the school counselor's erroneous conclusions.

The resistance of counselors to learning effective ways of helping Muslim clients is due mainly to negative feelings and attitudes toward Muslims, an assumption of the superiority of Western values and of the necessity to impose such values for the benefit of their clients, and finally the lack of incentive from institutions given to counselors to enhance their effectiveness with various cultural groups, particularly Muslims, through education and training.

"Multicultural counseling" education has increased considerably in the two decades separating Mr. Jones and Ms. Field. Whereas in the late 1970s and early 1980s only a small percentage of counseling programs required a multicultural counseling course, recent surveys show that 42 to 59 percent (Hills & Strozier, 1992; Quintana & Bernal, 1995) require such a course and that most programs have one or more elective courses in the area (Ponterotto et al., 1995). Jackson (1995) also states, "The 1980s and 1990s witnessed unprecedented growth in the specialty of multicultural counseling" (p. 12). Such growth did not begin until minority groups began to demand attention to their concerns (Jackson, 1995).

In disasters of various kinds, Muslims are often ignored, although they are likely to be among the victims or the victims' families who need attention and support. There are many striking illustrations of this unintentional negligence of the Muslim population. For instance, while many

Muslims and Arabs were killed in the hijacked planes and the World Trade Center in the terrorist attacks of September 11, 2001, most people were busy blaming Muslims rather than helping the victims' families. Ironically, a Muslim man from New Jersey who was killed in the attack on the World Trade Center after he rushed to help save lives was reported as a missing suspect. Several months later, his remains were discovered, and witnesses testified that they saw him running to the scene after the attacks out of patriotism and concern for fellow citizens. High-ranking government officials, including the mayor of New York City, went to his funeral and honored him for his patriotism and heroism. In transportation accidents, such as those involving trains, buses, and airplanes, Muslims can also be victims like all other groups. In some cases, they constitute the majority of victims. The crash of an Egyptian airliner off Nantucket Island, Massachusetts, on October 31, 1999, killing all 217 passengers aboard, provides evidence for both the need for multicultural competence in counseling and the urgency of including Muslims in it. The multinational passengers of the plane were categorized as follows: 106 Americans, 62 Egyptians, 22 Canadians, 3 Syrians, 2 Sudanese, 1 Chilean, and 3 unknown in addition to 18 Egyptian crew members. In addition to the victims with Arab nationalities who were mainly Muslims, a large number of the Americans as well as the Canadians were also Muslims who had become U.S. and Canadian citizens. Counseling the grieving families must have warranted the presence of counselors qualified and competent to counsel Muslims. In addition, in natural disasters such as hurricanes, storms, tornadoes, and earthquakes in the United States, the masses of people displaced from their homes and suffering the damages and destruction are likely to include Muslim victims. This warrants the inclusion of Muslims in counseling and relief efforts as well as the inclusion of these issues (i.e., natural disasters and plane crashes) in the list of issues that are facing American Muslims.

Mr. Jones admitted that he received no education or training on working with Muslims. Ms. Field describes her exposure to issues of multiculturalism: "In my master's training, the issues of multiculturalism were very strong in the program. They made students very aware of the concerns and the need to be aware of cultural differences between people." Although she studied various minority groups, including African Americans, Asian Americans, Indians, and Hispanics, her studies did not include Muslims. This was due not to a lack of textual information but rather to the lack of time. She explains, "They [Muslims] were in the book but we did not cover it."

It is not known why the instructor of the course dismissed the discussion of information related to Muslims in class. Whatever his or her reasons may have been, not teaching about a minority group by at least assigning readings that are readily available in a textbook suggests a high level of prejudice, or ignorance, and/or incompetence. Either way, the situation is alarming.

Mr. Jones and Ms. Field share more than their profession. Both work in public institutions: a community health center and a public middle school, respectively. In these two public institutions, clients have no other choice but to be counseled by these two counselors if they are referred for counseling. This is what I call "forced or mandated counseling or therapy." This type of counseling is required in schools and public health facilities and is mandated by the court system. The community center where Mr. Jones works is located in a low-income neighborhood that is heavily populated with a relatively large number of Muslims, particularly of African American descent. The school in which Ms. Field worked and trained as a school psychologist also has a relatively large number of students from the Arab and Arab–Muslim communities.

While one of our two counselors had no formal education or training in multiculturalism at all, the other had some multicultural education, but not in relation to Muslims. Nevertheless, both were sympathetic to the cause. Mr. Jones admitted that in many cases he was unable to resolve family issues, including husband–wife and child–parent relationships. He also learned from the families he met that both their religion and their culture (particularly Arabic) were not respected in their life experiences. His clients ended the sessions abruptly. Mr. Jones was reluctant to give any details for the fear of breaching the confidentiality of his clients.

Ms. Field, on the other hand, understood her limitations and obtained the consent of the family as well as the permission of the school district to involve me in the counseling of the two Muslim and Arab girls in her school. Obtaining the family's consent was very difficult as she described it. Obtaining the approval from the school's officials proved to be even more difficult. Ms. Field explains,

It's frustrating as a person in my position. I have some awareness of the importance of diversity and how it affects development and the impact it has on people's lives, and mine (i.e. awareness) is only minimum. And then there are people who have absolutely no awareness and they work with kids every day, and it is very hard for me to work with them (i.e. school's administrators, counselors and staff). In a school system it's important for everybody to work together, and it's difficult to do that when the awareness isn't there all around.

The Multiculturally Competent Counselor

The Sue, Arredondo, and McDavis (1992) model focuses on three main characteristics that have been determined as standards for multicultural competencies: (a) the counselor's awareness of his or her own assumptions, values, and biases; (b) the understanding of the worldview of the culturally different client; and (c) the development of appropriate intervention strategies and techniques. Each characteristic would be described as having three dimensions: beliefs and attitudes, knowledge, and skills.

If the need for multicultural awareness, education, and training is recognized as essential for effective counseling, why is it not then stipulated as an essential element of graduation and licensing requirements, especially for counselors working with minorities? Neither Ms. Field nor her colleague, the permanent counselor of the school, had any formal education or training in how to work with Muslims before they had their first encounter. D'Andrea and Daniels (1995) recommend establishing the principles of multicultural counseling as the centerpiece of the ethical standards of the counseling profession.

According to Sue et al. (1992), a body of literature exists documenting the widespread ineffectiveness of traditional counseling approaches and techniques when applied to racial and ethnic minority populations. The monocultural education and training most counselors receive has not been very useful. In the case of Ms. Field, as a student of multiculturalism, the instructor skipped the readings related to Muslims and Arabs as if it would be unlikely that students would encounter clients who are Arabs or Muslims. Furthermore, she also indicated that the multicultural training that she received on other minority groups is not adequate and, therefore, that it does not qualify her to work with members of such groups without her going back to her notes and participating in ongoing training. She suggested, therefore, that constant multicultural training set up at regular intervals would be ideal and most helpful.

An additional limitation that we must take into consideration is the lack of literature, studies, and research on Arabs and Muslims related to the field of counseling, especially in particular circumstances, such as issues of career counseling, cultural adjustment, and interfaith marriages. Until sufficient research is done and information is made available, it would, therefore, be extremely useful if professionals were directed to seek help from Muslim and Arab professionals or representatives of religious, educational, political, or cultural organizations without, of course, breaching the confidence of their clients.

Examination of Multicultural Competencies and the Standard Model

According to this model, counselors are required not only to know about their clients' cultural heritage but also to learn about how their own cultural heritage, education, and backgrounds affect their view of the world and their treatment of their culturally different clients. The counselors' own cultural heritage in relation to Muslims and Arabs may have been influenced, among other things, by (a) their own cultural assumption of superiority, (b) the underlying Euro-American-centric values of counseling professions, and (c) the widespread biases, assumptions, judgments, and attitudes with respect to Islam, Muslims, Arabs, and immigrants.

Acknowledging the limitations in understanding the worldview of Muslim clients that restrict counselors' ability to effectively work with them must be a high priority for counselors. This acknowledgment will encourage counselors to make referrals and to seek consultations with appropriate resources when the need arises.

Counselors also need to know the detrimental influence of racism in schools, in employment, and in the public treatment of Muslims and the ways in which it is affecting their clients. Counselors should, therefore, not only feel comfortable with their clients' differences but also be able to advocate for their clients and attempt to change the oppressive environment, policies, and settings in order to accommodate their clients' needs. If they do not do so, they will fail personally as well as professionally (Pedersen, 1988).

As I demonstrated earlier, current testing is a biased, unfair, and inaccurate method for the measurement of Muslim clients in school, college, and career counseling. Furthermore, testing is also biased in the determination of normal and abnormal behaviors and mental condition of Muslim clients. It is, therefore, a professional attribute not to rely on tests and assessment tools that are biased and unfair. Counselors may either search for unconventional assessment tools that are appropriate for the particular culture of the client or seek the input of culturally aware professionals to adjust the existing tools to be able to test what they claim to test.

Clients

Ms. Field describes both Amal and Mawrah, the two Palestinian American girls, as follows:

They're different. They're different than the majority of the kids in the school and I think the other kids in the school know that. A lot of the kids in the school don't understand why their parents, or their mother dresses the way that she does, because the parents have come to school and the mother dresses in the full clothing and I'm sure the kids ask the girls, "Why does she dress like that?" and those types of issues.

After meeting with the family and interviewing the father, the two girls, and their brother, who was a junior in high school, I found that the family's insistence on strictly adhering to the norms of their Palestinian culture was mainly due to the following reasons:

(a) It is perceived as the only way to maintain control over their children and ensure that they are holding on to the parents' traditional values while growing. It is customary in Arab culture, as it is in any collectivist society, that parents and teachers believe in one way of living and reject or fight against any deviation from their way. Studies and research show that parents of this culture (Palestinian) do not tolerate children's behavior that does not match their expectations (Dwairy, 1998). Furthermore, silencing could be imposed here as a means of control (Wadley, 1994).

(b) As I stated earlier, honor and family reputation are of utmost importance to Arabs. The family, therefore, informed me that they had instructed these attractive adolescent girls not to engage in any discussion, educationally oriented or otherwise, with males, including teachers. The girls were very smart, but because of this cultural attitude, they were not responding orally or otherwise to the instructions of their male teachers. As a result, they were diagnosed as retarded and consequently were assigned to special education classes. The problem was exacerbated because the girls were separately assigned to special education classes. Each of the girls was, therefore, called out of her classroom to go to a different room where she alone met with the teacher, who happened to be a male. The girls reported feeling very uncomfortable and even furious and consequently refused to communicate with their teachers.

(c) The Palestinian–Israeli conflict, with the involvement of the United States in support of Israel, helped institutionalize the fear of American culture and the view of it as antagonistic and unfriendly. The children—both girls and the high school boy—reported acts of discrimination from students as well as from staff. The high school boy reported that his counselor intentionally neglected him when he asked for academic guidance and sometimes was refused explicitly. The three children reported hearing anti-Arab and anti-Muslim remarks from students. When asked if they have reported these incidents to teachers and school administration, they said that they did but that it did not change anything. The boy would sometimes respond, which would lead him into physical fights with other students. The girls learned to withdraw and keep to themselves. They also reported that there is a negative portrayal of Islam and Arabic cultures in the educational materials and classroom discussions. Challenges such as these have a negative impact on individuals as well as societies. Haddad (1998) states,

> The American experience forges as well as forces a new Muslim identity that is born of both the quest to belong and the experience of being permanently depicted as "the other." As one young Muslim said, "I cannot be a white Anglo Protestant, but I have to be something. Every one has an identity. People keep asking: 'What are you?' 'What do you believe?' 'Why does Islam oppress women?' 'Why do you marry four wives?' 'Why does your religion teach violence?' Suddenly you begin to realize that you do not know what a Muslim is and you begin to search for yourself." (p. 33)

Supporting the existence of identity crisis among young American Muslims, Ms. Field states, "Who are they? Are they Americans? Or are they American-Muslims? Are they strictly Muslims? I don't know if they know who they are and where they fit in to the culture, because the values are so different in the population they're in. The school that they're in is very mono-cultural. It is not multicultural."

Ms. Field agrees that withdrawal from peers would also be an issue. She states. "I think the isolation from the other peers would probably be a problem."

The seriousness of the problem intensifies when we realize that cultural conflict and identity crises are not peculiar to Muslims; they are facing almost every minority group. Ms. Field says, "I have a third grade girl who is Asian-Indian, who comes to me every day crying because kids are making fun of her. So, I think it depends on the school environment that you're in. I am in a very suburban, white, middle-class American school system that isn't used to diversity."

The Counselor–Client Relationship

Ms. Field reported difficulty in establishing rapport with the family. Furthermore, she felt that they were resistant to counseling. Although she realizes the importance of a positive counseling relationship, she could not develop it.

Ms. Field explains, "I think developing relationships with the families is really important. It's difficult, but I think it's important."

When asked about whether it was difficult with one parent more than the other, she said, "It is equally as difficult, because the father spoke more English than the mother, but the father's personality was just so shut down and serious, that it was hard for me to deal with that."

It should be noted that unsuccessful attempts to establish rapport with clients and their families are not all the clients' fault. Counselors must be skillfully able to earn the trust of resistant clients. To Muslim clients, it would be immensely helpful if counselors assure them of understanding, safety, and support. One of the issues the parents raised as a reason for not cooperating with the counselor is that they were summoned to counseling in a language that they felt as threatening and humiliating.

Cultural Conflict at Its Peak

Ms. Field arranged for a meeting for the family with her in the presence of representatives from the school's administration, counseling office staff, and myself. The issues presented in the meeting were the following:

(a) Parents' lack of response to the school's request. The reason for citing such a concern is that one of the girls was diagnosed as nearsighted and in need of glasses. Parents were notified, but for almost four years they did not get glasses for her. Ms. Field attributed this to deficiency in understanding the English language, lack of cooperation, lack of concern, and possibly miscommunication. Ms. Field states,

[She] needed glasses, and that's been happening for four years now. I know that if money is an issue, if money is (claimed as) the reason the girl hasn't gotten glasses yet, I don't think that is the issue because I know that they qualify to receive benefits because the girls are identified as students in need of special education services. I don't think that they understand how to fill the forms to get this Medicaid money. So that may be interfering with the girl actually getting glasses, because the parents don't understand the whole concept.

In fact, it is the school and Ms. Field who do not understand the whole concept. When I interviewed the parents and the girl, I found that the father and all the children speak and understand English fluently. It was only the mother who did not speak or understand the language as fluently as the rest of the family did. The father understood well that his daughter needed glasses, and the family intentionally did not react. Their point was that

this is a young girl who will not continue her education. She'll get married as soon as her age allows. Having glasses for her may weaken her sight further. Furthermore, it may prevent her from getting married because who wants to marry a woman with weak sight. When they asked for glasses for my son I got it the same day. Money is not a problem. But look at him, his sight is much weaker now but, at least, he is a boy. (translated)

This statement clearly indicates that cultural beliefs, perhaps faulty ones, are affecting the girls' lives. While showing a willingness to continue education of the boy up until college, they did not want the girls to be educated beyond the level required by the law. In some traditional Arab customs, girls are deprived of education and other activities for the fear of doing something that brings shame to the whole family. In such customs, it is also believed that education is needed only to get a job or to attain a status belonging to males, but for women such accomplishments are unnecessary and undesirable.

(b) The girls' lack of participation and comprehension. Another issue brought up at the meeting was that the school speech therapist diagnosed the two girls as having a speech impairment. Ms. Field stated, "Well, according to the speech therapist, it's a language impairment, and not in the sense of—they have a different language—that's not it; their whole language processing. Their whole processing of the English language is deficient. There are students who have English as their second language who are able to process both their primary language and English as a second language okay. These girls are unable to do that."

When Ms. Field was asked if the therapist's diagnosis could be biased or influenced by cultural factors, she rejected that notion, saying, "The speech therapist said that it's not only because of the language—that there are some other types of processing deficits that they're going through. Even in nonverbal types of tasks that I do with them, I still see the same types of things that are typical of other kids who speak only English, but are language disabled."

It is apparent from this statement that Ms. Field, the counselor, has adopted the therapist's misdiagnosis. I call it misdiagnosis because it uses a form of standardized tests that are considered by experts to be biased and unfair especially to minority persons, and because the counselor's determination that the girls must be also deficient in the Arabic language as well was a gross mistake because the therapist did not consider using translation as a possibility to reach an accurate diagnosis. The future of these two girls did not seem important enough to make the effort to seek additional resources other than himself and the standardized tests he has. When I asked Ms. Field to describe the test, she said, "There was a lot of stuff with blocks. There are 12 different subtests—different tasks that you do with them." I further asked whether the girls understood the instructions and whether the therapist thought of using translations to Arabic. Ms. Field responded, "No. That was the other problem. That's one of the reasons I contacted you, because I was trying to figure out whether I should have it done that way or not. The speech therapist said, 'No.' They've said that English is their primary language, so they should be able to do these things in English. So that was the first point, when I said I have to ask somebody else—someone who knows."

When I met with the family and the committee, the family resented labeling their daughters "handicapped" and "disabled." Furthermore, they mentioned that their daughters speak English at home more than they do Arabic. The girls' admission that English is their primary language and the parents' agreement to that in the meeting were confirmed when I met personally with the girls and got to chat with them. I found them highly intelligent, responsive, and spontaneous. My assessment proved true when the two girls began communicating with teachers and classmates without fear or intimidation. Special education classes proved unnecessary and unneeded.

Conclusion of the Case

The dilemma of these two young girls had a happy ending. This was because of the efforts of Ms. Field and, as she expressed, her struggle to include an expert who was able to facilitate communication as well as bring about cultural understanding between the family and the girls on the one hand and the school's staff and counselors on the other. As a result of the meetings with the family and the school's administration and counseling staff, all issues were resolved as follows:

• The family agreed to obtain prescription glasses for their daughter.
• The school understood the complication of male–female relations in the Arab culture and agreed to make accommodations.
• The family agreed to allow their daughters to genuinely participate in their classroom discussions. Furthermore, they showed understanding and appreciation for girls' education so that they could realize their potentials.

On this unexpected conclusion, the author received a thank-you letter from Ms. Field on the formal letterhead of the school district. In it, Ms. Field admits that "it was fairly obvious that the language differences between the school staff and the [family] have been a barrier to accurate communication among all those involved. The concerns of the parents and the cultural influences on the girl's education would have continued to go unnoticed had it not been for your assistance."

Although Ms. Field attempted and made efforts to seek understanding and awareness, it is apparent that she, too, overestimated the expertise of her colleague, the speech therapist. His limitations in education, training, and familiarity with the population in part are due to working in an environment that is dominated by whites as well as the limitations in recognizing the biases of the tests used. Furthermore, Ms. Field indicated that she was fighting alone against all the school staff, who did not want to include an "outsider" even if such involvement was necessary and warranted because of the ongoing crisis in dealing with these two girls. This is not, by any means, an isolated case but rather the norm. It seems that institutions place guarding their internal integrity higher on the list of their priorities than their duty to accommodate the needs of their constituencies that make their services, education in this case, effective and more beneficial.

This case is also indicative of the fact that lack of awareness of the culture of the clients and the level to which these cultures affect their clients' perceptions are but two factors of conflict in cultural communication that counselors frequently face. In the case of Muslims, religion may also play an important role in complicating the issues they face and in the way they can be resolved. In summation, this model of counseling and several other models fail to include the importance of religion and culture in the counseling of clients, the biases in standardized assessment and testing, and what counselors need to do in order to overcome such biases. Furthermore, this model fails to encourage counselors to take advantage of traditional forms of support and counseling that may have roots in the cultures of their minority clients.

DISCUSSION AND IMPLICATIONS

The counseling profession is expanding to include areas of life that have never been included in counseling before. A good example of that is Reitmeyer's (2000) article "Dog Gone? From Cats to Snakes, Counselors Help Heal Human Hearts Following Loss of a Pet." On the one hand, this article shows concern for individuals who are grieving for pet loss and attempts to provide insight for "healing their hearts." On the other hand, it demonstrates that similar attempts have not been made to help the Muslim minority deal with various issues, including those of grief and loss. In order to better understand the needs of Muslim clients, counselors are urged to do the following:

- Understand and develop the awareness of their own cultural heritage and how can it affect their dealing with Muslim clients
- Understand the worldview of their Muslim clients, including both cultural and religious influences
- Assess the personal, cultural, and religious identity of their clients
- Understand the limitations and biases of testing and attempt to change the contents or modify them to fairly represent the areas intended for testing
- Use all resources available for consultation to ensure the full benefit of the client
- In case they are not able to help the client, use referrals to more experienced counselors
- Help the client understand the purpose and what he or she can expect of the counseling relationship
- If the issue is religious, ensure the client that his or her religious principles and values are respected and try to help the client through consultation, referrals, or the involvement of a third party with the client's consent

Since the Sue et al. (1992) model encourages counselors to develop understanding and awareness of the cultural background of the client, information given in this book can help one develop an awareness of Muslim clients' general culture, general subculture, level of acculturation, level of religiosity, and personal needs and wants. If either the issue or the person is religious, the client may be surveyed to see whether he or she prefers interventions from a religious figure or a person who has knowledge of Islam. Often the client may not want to involve a member of the Islamic community for a variety of reasons, including the fear of being exposed or feeling ashamed. The counselor's knowledge of Islam, whether previously acquired or acquired only for the purpose of this particular case from credible sources, will be of utmost benefit.

Until now, culturally different clients have been left to the mercy and kindness of the therapist in the sense that no competencies and standards are required for licensing by the American Counseling Association (ACA), CACREP, or any other national or local institutions. If this practice is allowed in individual counseling practices, it must not be tolerated if the counselor or therapist is going to work in schools, courts, mental health institutions, or public health facilities, which are naturally diverse. Multicultural competencies must, therefore, be included in education and professional training programs and must be required of therapists who intend to work in multicultural sittings. From my academic studies, I remember that multicultural courses and specialization were made optional. They should be mandatory for counselors and therapists to receive accreditation and licensing to work with the population they intend to serve. This may open the door for specialization in psychotherapy as it is in the medical field, a welcomed innovation indeed. Training must be frequent and periodic. This will serve as a reminder and, at the same time, will allow therapists to be informed about new issues and developments. In associations such as the ACA and ARVIC, representation for Arab and Muslim cultures must be included.

QUESTIONS FOR DISCUSSION

1. How do you view the level of accommodation to different cultures in the origin and underlying philosophy of Western counseling?
2. What are the implications of the insensitive use of Western counseling on the culturally different client?
3. What are the criteria for good counseling in general, according to the author, and for Muslim clients in particular?

CHAPTER 5

Counseling through the Eyes of Muslims

In this chapter, I examine the decision-making process among Muslim families with respect to seeking counseling, the criteria of selecting counselors, and the factors that help make counseling successful.

COUNSELING BY REQUEST ONLY

Except for Wahida (a white American woman) and the Hikmats, none of the clients sought counseling or therapy on his or her own. Hikmat's family is different from other clients in two ways: the Hikmats have had a longer stay in the United States than other clients (over 25 years), and the husband has a postgraduate degree (a Ph.D.). Such difference in attitudes toward counseling indicate that education in U.S. institutions, a long time of residence in the United States, and consequently a long time in a typical American workplace environment are among the factors that speed up the process of acculturation and assimilation and consequently the willingness to seek counseling when needed. Several Arab communities that live in the United States and work as cultural groups (e.g., in Lakawana, New York, and Dearborn, Michigan) have little, if any, contact with other groups and cultures. Such groups are likely to resist acculturation for a longer time than the other groups that work and mix with other cultures.

Other clients sought counseling only when requested by a significant family member (e.g., a parent or a spouse), a medical health professional, a court judge, a social worker, a school administrator, a teacher, or a counselor. Farida brought her husband to family counseling as a result of the therapist's request. Child rearing is viewed in patriarchal societies as a woman's responsibility, and this may explain the reluctance of Farida's husband to learn in therapy sessions how to deal with and handle the needs of his disabled child.

The first response to the request of relatives or others for counseling was resistance and opposition. Clients' reluctance led to an unnecessary delay in counseling. Farida, for instance, waited for three years before seeing a therapist. She went to a therapist only on the referral of her son's social worker. When asked whether she sought help of any sort before going to therapy, she answered,

Not really—mostly talking to friends about it and talking to doctors, like when I called twice a day to ask about something he did or some kind of symptoms he had, or the therapist used to come to him [the physical therapist]—they told me once, "You've got to stop calling us two, three times a day, because you don't have to ask about every move he does." Then I realized I need someone to talk to.

It is true that Muslims in general draw great support and strength from extended family members, something that most Muslims in the United States do not necessarily have. On the one hand, families of immigrant backgrounds may not have had the opportunity to enjoy the company of the members of their extended families for a wide range of reasons, including immigration laws, employment opportunities, and cultural or personal preferences of family members. On the other hand, Muslim converts may have lost the support of their extended families, if they had any, as a result of their conversion.

This suggests that the absence of strong family support among American Muslims after having been accustomed to it makes the need for counseling, therapy, and support groups even greater.

In the case of the Hikmat family, they sought counseling only when they felt that the problems they were having were beyond their abilities to handle. Furthermore, they were unable to sort out such problems by themselves, and consequently the family ties became at risk. Hikmat explains, "We almost started blaming each other—who did what which brought her [their daughter] to that point. So that was actually affecting our own relationship and we started drifting apart from each other and blaming each other. So that was the time that we felt that we actually needed counseling to really sort it out before it is too late."

Hikmat was encouraged even further when he learned through his job that expenses for counseling services were covered by his employment. Hikmat says, "So on one hand, having a problem for which we felt we needed a counselor to help us, and also on the other hand, knowing that the company had arranged for that kind of facility for their employees, we decided to take you up on that opportunity to help us."

Although the Hikmats consider themselves as higher middle class and as financially well off, the appeal of "free counseling" rather than the need for counseling seems to be the factor that played a greater role in seeking counseling. The level of acculturation only allowed them to go without personal or cultural resistance. This suggests that the benefits of counseling and therapy are not well known or publicized among the Muslim populations.

Who Makes the Decision?

Most Muslims are likely to reject the idea of counseling when it is suggested to them for the first time. Wahida and Farida, from among my clients, are the only exceptions to that rule. Wahida, because of her American background, was accustomed to counseling and therapy. Farida, the mother of a disabled child, was the one who insisted on going against the husband's opposition. Later on, the husband accepted. She describes the situation as follows:

Like when I started going to therapy myself, my husband didn't approve. My husband thinks that he is everything and you just be patient and don't give things more attention than you should. My husband was against my going to a therapist. He didn't say, "I'm not going to let you go," because the relationship between us was such that he wasn't giving me orders what to do and what not to do, but when I started going, he said, "If you feel better with doing that, go ahead." When I started the medication, too, he said, "No" at the beginning but then he said that it was okay if I felt better. He realized that I was doing better with the medication and the therapist.

To the contrary, Pride, in her first counseling experience, was referred by her doctor. Furthermore, her doctor's referral alone was not sufficient. In addition, she needed her husband's encouragement and permission to justify seeking counseling. The husband, who received his master's degree from a university in the United States, agreed to her going to counseling, according to Pride. The husband informed me later at a joint session that it was he who requested Pride to go to counseling, but she refused. This means that Pride needed both cultural validation as well as a medical referral in order to seek counseling. As soon as she obtained these, she began therapy. This means that neither the husband nor the doctor alone was sufficient for Pride to accept therapy. She confirms that by saying that she went to counseling only when she felt that "there is no other way except to go to counseling."

Labibah, the college student, went to counseling on her parents' demands. In high school, she was second best academically and was recognized as the salutatorian for her entire high school. After transferring between two reputable, prestigious, and expensive colleges, she decided to stay home and quit education altogether. By doing that, she felt that she would be more religious. Her parents were shocked to see their daughter's high educational ambitions and goals evaporate to the point where she was no longer interested in any form of education. Every time her parents attempted to convince her to resume her education, she would withdraw to the seclusion of her room for days or weeks. Her parents began to worry about her while at the same time expressing anger at her decision. They demanded that she go to counseling, but, unlike the Hikmats, they themselves did not seek counseling as a family. Labibah's resistance to counseling, which took place only on the insistence of her parents, may have been a result of her parents' negative view of counseling as manifested in not seeking it themselves. The refusal of Labibah's parents to seek counseling despite their need for it to learn, at least, to effectively communicate with their daughter and with each other may have signaled to Labibah that counseling equals punishment, and since she was the one to blame for quitting school, she was the one who must go.

As we have seen, the decision to seek counseling is not made by the person needing it. Rather, it is made for them by either a family member or an outsider who is an authority figure for the person or the family. Even then, there is a degree of reluctance to go through with it. This is likely to be representative of many members of the Muslim population.

Choosing a Counselor

Gender

The family unit is central to Islam, and relations between sexes are defined exclusively in terms of that unit (Haddad & Lummis, 1987). The two sexes can mix and interact freely with each other within certain close and first degree family ties. Families impose and observe strict rules on interaction between the sexes with strangers or other family members who are not very close. The limitations or the lack of limitations set on interactions between the sexes depend, therefore, on how religiously and culturally conservative or liberal the individual or family is. Factors related to the sex or gender of the counselor must, therefore, be considered. Whether the gender of a counselor constitutes a concern to Muslim clients seems to depend on three main factors: (a) the individual's own views in addition to his or her religious, social, and cultural beliefs, (b) the issues for which counseling is sought, and (c) the urgency of the situation for which counseling is needed.

Pride, for instance, a woman and a mother of five children, insisted on seeing a female counselor. I further asked Pride, "Why did you choose to go to a woman counselor?" She answered, "I would be more comfortable talking. Because I am a woman, so I'm more comfortable talking to a woman." Although Pride thinks that her preference for a woman stems from religion, her statement suggests that it could be more rooted in culture than religion. She states, "I am not used to talking to a man. I'm more comfortable with a woman. I'm not used to it [with a man]."

Furthermore, it also suggests that Pride was worried about her image in the community—that she does not want to be viewed as having compromised religious or cultural norms simply by going to a male therapist if it ever becomes known. In general, Muslim women, in both the religion and the many cultures of the Muslim world, are discouraged from mixing with men. In many Muslim cultures (e.g., the Gulf states and Saudi Arabia), girls and boys are educated in separate schools and institutions. In Saudi Arabia, women are not only separated in schools but also have their own banks, clinics, and other facilities. In Egypt, separation between the sexes is stronger in the schools of Al-Azhar, the famous and most prestigious 11-centuries-old Islamic University. This translates to the preference of many Muslim women to be treated by female medical professionals (e.g., physicians and nurses). This also holds true for psychiatrists, therapists, counselors, and other mental health professionals.

Adding Pride's experience to that of the two Palestinian Muslim girls who seemed unwilling to respond to their male teachers illustrates the common trend among Muslim clients, especially females, of a preference for female therapists and counselors. Labibah, the female college student, insisted on a female counselor. To many other Muslims, the gender of the counselor may not be an issue. This category may include Muslim individuals who have been accustomed to studying and/or working in mixed environments, particularly in an American context.

Hikmat expressed satisfaction in the second counseling experience with a female counselor after terminating the first counseling experience with a male counselor. Although he stated as the reason that the counselor was being judgmental, his statement revealed fear and threat to his authority. Hikmat states,

He made a judgment about the father's role in the family. He kind of led us to it—just like, you know how these days we hear there are kids who have never been abused, but a problem comes and they go to a counselor and the counselor made them believe [they have been] and they even make up a story. So, at times we didn't know. But when I think back I see that person didn't know, I don't think, he was purposely doing it, but he consciously or unconsciously led us to kind of blame each other, and not only each other but slowly and gradually putting all the blame pretty much on me. Because you think once a thing like that came, everybody could remember something which I might have unilaterally decided. So each of them could say, "Yah, Daddy does whatever he wants to do."

Hikmat's wife, Halimah, did not express discomfort for having received counseling by a man. Instead, she was apologetic for the counselor and expressed feelings of regret and disappointment for having terminated the sessions early. In contradiction to her husband's perception of the first counselor, she states, "I didn't feel that. I personally think that we did not give him enough time."

The reason for her sympathy is that she felt that it was their responsibility to figure out the problem before going to counseling. Halimah states, "I think maybe if we had gone three or four times, he would understand then what he should do. The second time [with the second counselor], it was like, 'This is the problem and please help us do something.' The first one [counselor] is, 'Well, we're having so many problems and I don't know what to do.'"

Having said that, the Arabic patriarchal cultures seem also to have affected women's confidence in the capability of women in general to handle difficult tasks or jobs. Although Farida's preferences depend on the issues of counseling as she said, her preference in general is for a male counselor because, as she said, "I prefer a man. I think a man is stronger to handle stress. . . . If I am going to talk about what used to happen between me and my husband, like in the bedroom, I would rather talk to a woman because I wouldn't be shy. But some other issues—no."

Because of personal as well as societal factors, the preference for same-sex professionals is more emphasized for women than it is for men. Although religiously both men and women have the same restrictions as well as allowances in seeking help and treatment, many Muslim cultures remain strongly conservative and restrictive with respect to women. This makes the task of men accessing help much easier than that of women. This is due in part to the fact that the pressure on women to adhere to societal norms is much greater than that on men. Other factors include the conviction of a woman regarding her beliefs, which may override her concerns for societal approval, and family structure, norms, and values, which are given much more consideration by women than by society at large. Among Muslims in the United States, the extended family of a female may not be in close proximity. This does not mean that she feels at liberty to make decisions on her own in the absence of authority figures in the family. This is due in essence to the fact that in most Muslim societies, a woman's reputation, being based on her conduct, may affect positively or negatively her future life, including marriage, status, and her relation to society at large.

In my own personal as well as professional experience, I have not seen many men who hesitate to seek treatment or any services because of the gender of the service provider. This is not the case for most women. It is not at all unusual to encounter a woman who refuses to seek medical treatment even at times of serious illness because the service provider is a male.

If counseling is in group sessions where the woman is alone behind closed doors with a male counselor, the Muslim woman is likely to accept male counselors without much resistance. If the counseling issues involve intimacy, emotions, or a relationship between spouses, a Muslim client is likely to prefer a counselor of the same sex.

For men, because Islam and consequently most of Muslim cultures are viewed as patriarchal, it is difficult and may be unusual for a male to complain or express weakness to a female counselor. A female Muslim client would be hesitant to express her intimate feelings to a male counselor as she commonly would discuss physical pain and complaints with a male physician.

In the case of religious clients, they are likely to see all issues as religious, thus observing the traditional gender rules of separation between men and women.

Related to the discussion on gender differences, some techniques in counseling may be considered inappropriate or even counterproductive with Muslim clients. For instance, eye contact, touching clients softly, and keeping close physical proximity, which are considered necessary in Western counseling as signs of warmth in the counseling relationship (Cormier & Cormier, 1990), may be interpreted by Muslim clients as sexual gestures and advances. In Islam, both men and women are instructed to lower their gaze and to stay away from nonrelated people of the opposite sex. Furthermore, the Council on American Islamic Relations (1997) states the following in its "Employer's Guide to Islamic Religious Practices": "Some Muslims will be reluctant to shake the hand of an unrelated person of the opposite sex. This should not be taken as an insult but as a sign of personal modesty."

On the other hand, counselors may misinterpret Muslims' attitudes of avoiding eye contact, touching, and distant physical proximity as coldness and resistance to counseling (Cormier & Cormier, 1990). Thus, it is clear that physical behavior and protocol are important for successful counseling.

Religion

Whether the religion of clients is important in their choice of a counselor depends on the client's religiosity and perception of counseling and the issues of counseling.

Although 92 percent of the people in the United States are affiliated with a religion (Kosmin & Lachman, 1993), the awareness of the need for a consideration of religious and spiritual roles in counseling is a recent development in the field (Constantine, 1999). In the general population, especially in minority groups, religious or special issues are often embedded within the issues that bring many racial and ethnic minority clients to counseling. In contrast, therapists tend to be much less religiously oriented than their clients (Bergin, 1980; Worthington, 1989).

Therefore, many people with emotional difficulties are, among other reasons, turning to their rabbis, priests, or ministers for assistance (Weaver, Koneig, & Larson, 1997). Imams should be added to the list of clergy members providing pastoral counseling. While many clergy have, in fact, expanded education and training to meet the demands of the new role of providing counseling—either as a part of, alongside, or independent of spiritual care—imams remain inadequately educated and trained in this field.

In the United States, because of the absence of professionals who perform essential services that are usually available in the Muslim world, such as *qadis* (judges), *ma'zuns* (marriage officiating officers), and *a'lims* (jurists), imams must be trained to meet such requirements.

Imams are usually helping new immigrants and refugees adjust to the new culture, providing family counseling, visiting the sick, and supporting the bereaved. Because most imams are doing these functions without systematic education or professional training, the level of their effectiveness is not comforting.

Haddad and Lummis (1987) record what one imam said:

The role of the imam in the United States is completely different from the role of the imam in the Muslim World. In the Muslim world the imam's job is just to lead the prayer, but when you come to the United States, the role of imam is several roles. For example, here the imam conducts the funerals, a job which the imam back home would not do. There is a special person authorized by the government to perform marriages. Here too the imam practices the job of a marriage counselor, or an arbitrator between husband and wife, parents and children. This role of course is not practiced by the imam in the Muslim world. The mosque in America serves the Muslim affairs from cradle to death . . . a place where . . . all the necessary functions of society—economic, political, social, religious . . . recreational—everything is being practiced here. The imam is the center for that place so he is the one to be involved with them, with all these things. (p. 56)

By declaring that the education and training of imams in pastoral counseling is necessary, I do not mean to suggest that all Muslim clients will necessarily favor going to an imam for counseling, at least not in all cases. Depending on the client and the issues, if the issue is not seen by the client as religiously based (e.g., family communication, academic or career counseling, job discrimination, or emotional attachment), he or she is likely to seek therapeutic, not religious, counseling. Furthermore, since most imams are neither formally educated nor trained as counselors and therapists, the only option most Muslims are left with is to seek help from professionally educated, trained, and experienced counselors and therapists.

An additional factor is that the imam's office is located in the mosque, a highly visible public place, thus raising concerns among clients about confidentiality and leading to anxiety or fear of being stigmatized by other members of the community or for being seen or observed going to the imam's office.

One might even go a step further to suggest that it is to the benefit of clients to separate the tasks of an imam from those of a counselor. The position of imam always implies power, authority, judgmental attitude, and some level of control on clients, all of which may be intimidating and thus hinder clients from getting the benefits of counseling they might get from professional counselors.

Describing her feelings toward me and her perception of me as a counselor, Pride states,

You were more understanding than what I thought. I thought you would be very angry. You are the imam and you [waving her fist] but you were not. You understand and you look more "Americanized."

The issue of power may occur in a different context. Since the imam's position is that of a hired employee and the work of the imam is supervised, monitored, and evaluated by a committee, the imam's influence may be diminished if the client is one who has power over the office of the imam itself. This conflict of authority is best illustrated by the following statement from a former member of the board at my place of employment. He states, "We thought of maybe going and discussing with you, but then we decided maybe we would be better off going to somebody who wouldn't know us personally and who would be—maybe more independent and unbiased in his analysis of a situation and also we were concerned that with our [official] relationship, you may not feel free enough to advise us what you might think would be necessary for us to listen."

The authority of the imam can, therefore, influence the client to a degree that is not healthy. At the same time, his advice can be influenced by the authority of his clients who play other roles in the affairs of the same religious community. Similar conflicts may include cases of personal friends, supervisors, board members, major donors, or even relatives who need counseling.

The separation between the two functions, therefore, will prove to be healthier and mutually beneficial. It will help the imam avoid conflict of values or interests and, at the same time, will not intimidate any individual or group from seeking counseling just because of a perceived or true image of the imam. This is precisely why the Muslim population is in tremendous need of more counselors, therapists, and social workers from among the members of the Islamic community itself. Recent history has seen the establishment of many associations for Muslim practitioners and professionals, the last of which is the Association of Muslim Social Services, which was established in September 1999 after several national meetings and conferences.

To illustrate Muslims' values as they relate to mental health, a survey was conducted in which clients were described as quite religious. Responses to the counselor preferences questions show that a slight majority (52.9 percent; $n = 64$) responded that if they needed counseling, they would prefer a Muslim counselor, whereas 43.8 percent ($n = 53$) responded that either a Muslim or a non-Muslim counselor would be acceptable. If they had to go to a non-Muslim counselor, over 50 percent of the respondents said that it was very important, and another 25 percent said that it is somewhat important, for the counselor to have an understanding of Islamic values (Kelly, Aridi, & Bakhtiar 1996, p. 211).

The views of my clients supported the findings of this survey. When the presenting issue of counseling is religious, all expressed strong support for going to a Muslim counselor. Hikmat's wife, Halimah, states, "Personally, I didn't know that there was some Muslim counselor; I would have gone to that person because they will understand more than any other religion. But at that time, the way I remember it, I didn't even know that there was any Muslim counselor. So, maybe my husband knew that, but I didn't."

Confidentiality

Other clients, like Farida, Labibah, and Pride, expressed that their main concern was confidentiality. If they go to a Muslim counselor, whether he was an imam or someone else, there is the fear of confidentiality being broken. This is due in part to the small size of Muslim communities where everyone knows everyone else. When asked whether she thought of going to a Muslim counselor before going to the one she went to, Labibah stated, "I had been told that in this area there was one, but there were questions about confidentiality. So it turned out that I would go to a non-Muslim."

Even when the Muslim counselor is not the imam or the clergy, the issue of confidentiality is of great concern because that counselor, male or female, is expected to socialize and have most of his or her friends from the generally small Muslim community. Although it is expected that a professional adheres to the codes of ethics of his or her profession, Muslims fear that going to a Muslim counselor may compromise their confidentiality. This is due to the sensitivity of mental health issues and to the stigma that surrounds them. Muslim physicians, for instance, do not face the same problem to the same level because physical illnesses do not have stigma attached to them as do counseling, therapy, and mental health issues.

It is for the same reason of confidentiality that Farida would not go to an Arab–Muslim therapist. When she was asked about whether a male could counsel her on women's issues, she answered, "I think he could, except if he is Arabic—no. If he is Arabic–Muslim I would not go to him as a counselor. That's a big issue."

Political Friend or Foe

Political factors, such as the Arab–Israeli and Bosnian–Serbian conflicts, also have their impact on the choice of a counselor by Muslim clients. Farida, for instance, who comes originally from Palestine, asserted that she would ask before going to the counselor if he is Jewish. It is obvious that Farida does not make the distinction between a Jew and a pro-Israeli. She says, "I always ask if it is a Jewish person. . . . I would feel more comfortable talking to a Christian person than a Jewish one." The same perception is expected to surface in the case of Bosnians who may be faced with a Serbian counselor.

Often clients do not have the leverage to choose their own counselors, such as in school counseling, court-mandated counseling, and so on. In such cases and if religion or political orientation is an issue, it would be wise to examine any objections or reservations the client may have and deal with them before the actual counseling begins. In such a case, counselors need to assure clients of sympathy, understanding, positive regard, and support without prejudice. Counselors neither have to adopt their clients' views nor dismiss their own. Rather, counselors have the obligation to assure their clients that their (the counselors) own religious or political views will not affect their professional attitude toward their clients.

GOOD COUNSELING ACCORDING TO MUSLIM CLIENTS

By "good counseling," I mean the elements of counseling that Muslim clients view as helpful, encouraging, and productive. These elements enable clients to continue the counseling after it has begun, cooperate with the counselor, and/or lead to desirable conclusions of the counseling relationship or to the issues of concern. At the same time, the opposites of these characteristics may be considered detrimental to counseling.

In this section, I use my clients' remarks to outline the preferred characteristics of the counselor of choice.

Positive Regard for the Client

Respect for the client is a very important element in the counseling process. It is, therefore, necessary for the counselor to (a) communicate willingness to work with the client, (b) show interest in the client as a person, and (c) convey acceptance of the client (Cormier & Cormier, 1991). My clients stressed that the counselor's positive attitude encouraged both openness on their part and continuity of counseling.

Pride, who was very hesitant and unwilling at first to seek counseling, felt encouraged to open up to a stranger (i.e., the counselor) from the start; this, in turn, made her feel better. She described the counselor as "listening": "she was part of me." She states, "She was 'proud' of me—to say [to open up]—that the first time I saw her I was able to tell her about my problems. It's not easy to come out, the first time."

In general terms, the counselor needs to demonstrate positive regard to the clients. Farida states,

Well, first of all, he has to be patient—very patient, because you're not going to go there, the first time you meet a person, and tell him everything about your life. You've got to trust him. I mean, he has to be compassionate and loving and he has to have good qualities for me to trust him and to feel comfortable about him, I mean, the tone of his voice, the way he gestures, the way he talks to me, the way he answers my questions—I mean, if he's mean or rude or laughs at me or he doesn't take me seriously, I would go.

Counselor Is Nonjudgmental

The Hikmat family stopped going to their first counselor because he started blaming the husband as the dominant dictatorship figure in the family. To the contrary, their second counselor attentively listened and expressed sympathy to the whole family without being judgmental. This attitude encouraged the family to continue and led counseling to a happy end. Hikmat describes his experience with the second counselor as follows:

And even the way she made me think. I used to blame myself for everything—like with what happened to my daughter, I'd say, "Oh my God, I think because I used to talk about diets so much and maybe that is why she got into that." And she [the counselor] said, "Why do you blame yourself?" Anything that would happen, I would say, "Maybe I did that or I didn't raise her good maybe I did something." And she'd try to tell me, "Don't blame yourself all the time, because everyone has a responsibility, especially when they're older. They should know what's wrong and what's right. Don't blame yourself."

Counselor Acknowledges Limitations

While being counseled for the emotional stress and grief that resulted from the murder of her husband, Farida also had religious concerns, such as whether her husband was going to heaven or hell and whether she had been a good wife to her husband. The counselor attempted to comfort her by telling her that he must now be in heaven. Knowing that the counselor was not a Muslim and had limited, if any, knowledge about Islam, Farida's response to the counselor was, "How would you know that my husband is in heaven?" Farida was concerned for her husband, a grocery store owner who used to sell beer, tobacco, pork, and lottery tickets, all of which are unlawful in Islam. The concern of Farida was that God may be punishing him now for his violations of Islamic principles.

The simplistic and rather naive answers were but a demonstration of the counselor's lack of credibility, which in turn furthered and intensified Farida's anguish and grief. In addition, Farida complained of feelings of "big guilt," as she described: "Most of the time when I was there we were talking about how guilty sometimes the person who is left can feel about [times] when I used to fight with my husband and I used to tell him not to do this or that. It was mostly about the guilt the person feels and the emptiness and loneliness the person feels and my being scared of guns and violence and teenagers."

All these issues required the counselor's awareness of religious as well as cultural backgrounds and beliefs. Farida, an Arab Muslim, felt mandated by both Arabic culture and religion of Islam to be obedient and submissive to her husband. The counselor disregarded all the feelings of guilt, fear, emptiness, and loneliness that almost crippled Farida. Mere advice to Farida to look through the window and see the birds singing and flying from tree to tree did not prove helpful. Furthermore, the counselor admonished Farida that looking back would not change her situation.

It may have been more helpful to Farida to have been reminded of the Islamic belief of the unlimited and vast mercy of God. Asking her to mention the good things her husband used to do (e.g., support the family, act kindly to others, and practice his religion) would have helped her value the religiosity of her husband. In Islam, the reward is not limited to rituals and acts of worship; rather, everything we do can be rewarded by God as an act of worship that opens the door to multiple rewards. When the counselor contacted me, I advised him to involve me officially in the case if Farida agreed. When Farida came to see me, she told me that she stopped seeing that counselor completely because he was not well informed.

To the contrary, the Hikmats appreciated their second counselor when that counselor acknowledged her limitations in dealing with eating disorders. While referring them to a specialist, she helped the family establish better communication and stronger relationships among its members.

The Counselor's Experience

Most clients preferred that the counselor be between 40 and 60 years of age. To them, this age represented more experience. Farida's reasoning is as follows:

I think they have more experience in life. They will be studying more. . . . They should because they saw so many people before me. If it's someone who just started, I don't think he would have the same experience, like one with an older age. Like the one I go to, he said, "I have been doing this for 22 years"—or since he was 22, and he's 60 now. That's 40 years. I mean, he's definitely going to be better than the one who just started.

In addition to seniority, clients develop trust in the counselor based on the perception of counselor's expertness. This perception can be enhanced by the counselor's apparent level of skill, relevant education, specialized training or experience, certificates or licenses, status, type of setting in which the counselor works, history of success in solving the problems of others, and the counselor's ascribed role as a helper (Cormier & Cormier, 1991). Some of these elements can be seen while others must be ascertained by the counselor.

It would, therefore, be helpful to Muslim clients if the counselors informed their clients of their educational background, of their general knowledge of Muslim cultures, and of any special training they might have had with respect to Muslims. Also of great value is the emphasis of the counselor on the cases of success he or she had in working with Muslims and the counselor's demonstration of understanding and respect for Muslims' values.

BAD COUNSELING ACCORDING TO MUSLIM CLIENTS

The following issues constituted to clients what they labeled as bad counseling. By "bad counseling," I mean the experience that has led a client to terminate the counseling relationship prematurely, discouraged clients from seeking counseling again, or did not help the clients sort out their problems and consequently solve them. These factors are equally considered inhibitors to effective counseling among the Muslim population.

Counselor's Appearance

The counselor's appearance in the initial session creates an important first impression with clients. After she quit her first counselor because of her inability to pay for the sessions, Farida searched for a counselor who would accept Medicaid payments. Farida describes the counselor she found as follows: "I didn't like the way she looked. She's not a clean person. I mean, the way she dressed, she's awful. I felt like I have to tell her what to do instead of her telling me what to do."

Neat, formal dressing would encourage clients who are very particular and meticulous about appearance. Sloppy dressing, as well as the displaying of pop-culture influence (e.g., body piercing, tattoos, strange hair-styles and colors, and so on) would be a turnoff for a Muslim client. It is also apparent from Farida's statement that she viewed the counselor as a person of influence who, therefore, must be able to earn the client's respect.

A related issue is general hygiene and the organization and odor of the counselor's office. Farida's feelings of disgust that resulted from the coun-selor's appearance were intensified by the odor of the food that the coun-selor kept in the drawers of her desk. Farida states, "Yah, and she wasn't a clean person. She had like a bunch of food in her drawers and the food smelled."

To the contrary, Pride was encouraged by the counselor's formal dress, the cleanliness of her office, and the organization of her desk and room. Linking the good dressing with the effectiveness of counseling strategies and techniques, Pride states, "She was a lady, good looking. She was nice. . . . She was one who listens to me in every situation."

Furthermore, some clients may judge the counselor's personality on the basis of the way he or she dresses. Pride states, "She wore a skirt and a blouse, with normal buttons. For me, the personality is very important. If I see someone—if I don't like their personality—I don't go to them, but she's okay. She's not perfect, but she's okay."

Too formal dress, however, may be a turnoff to others because of the image it portrays of authority, formality, and distance. Pride describes this by saying, "Because . . . I don't want to see someone dressed sloppy. She was dressed 'normal.' She is not too much like an educated person. She was more ordinary."

Perceiving formal dress as a sign of high education may be rooted in Pride's culture. Although education itself is desirable for both the coun-selor and the client, attitudes of arrogance and superiority that some educated people display are not. Therefore, Pride's expression serves to illustrate the preference among Muslim clients for the qualities of modesty and humbleness, which are encouraged by Islam and many Eastern and Arab cultures. When a Muslim client denies his or her expertise on a particular subject, he or she may be doing so out of humbleness and not from the real lack of such experience.

Counselor Is Judgmental

The negative assessment that the Hikmat family made of their first counseling experience resulted from the counselor's judgmental attitude against the father as the source of the problem. The family was worried that he might end up convincing the children of things that never hap-pened under the label of "repressed memories," the validity of which is greatly disputed. In widely publicized and controversial court cases, several children were made to believe in the occurrence of abuse while, in fact, it never happened. Hikmat states, "That person, rather than understanding the problem, he made us fight ... and he just created other problems."

It is very important, therefore, that counselors first help clients identify the problem before they judge, blame, or put conditions on the clients to change their customs or beliefs in order to achieve results and then assure clients of neutrality and respect. From the first session, Hikmat declared that the counselor was biased against him as a male figure. The mere disagreement of the husband and wife over the effectiveness of the first counselor in the interviews is in itself a manifestation of opposing viewpoints within this particular family. It is, therefore, necessary to study the unique dynamics within each family and to respect such dynamics. Counselors must not attempt to change the family dynamic of their clients unless they themselves express both a desire and a willingness to change. Otherwise, the counselor is likely to create more conflicts rather than solve existing ones.

The majority of American Muslims, being of immigrant origin, are likely to feel that the extended family system is the normal and only acceptable support system. Among the most widely spread biased assumptions in the counseling profession are the assumption that there must be only one measure of "normal" that all people must share and that "individuals" are the basic blocks of society (Pedersen, 1988). Being nonjudgmental means that the counselor warmly accepts the client's expressions and experiences without expressing disapproval or criticism. A nonjudgmental attitude is defined according to Cormier and Cormier (1990) as "[t]he counselor's capacity to suspend judgment of the client's actions or motives and to avoid condemning or condoning the client's thoughts, feelings, or actions. It may also be described as the counselor's acceptance of the client without conditions or reservations, although it does not mean that the counselor supports or agrees with all the client says or does" (p. 29).

Counselor Is Uninformative and/or Untrustworthy

When Labibah visited her first and last counselor for the first time, her apprehension with respect to counseling and therapy led her to terminate the counseling relationship. She found her negative expectations true when the counselor began a session of interrogation, as she described it, without informing her as to what the procedure would entail and what she should expect. What the counselor should have done first was to establish rapport and inform the client about her strategies, techniques, and approaches and how the client could cooperate to facilitate the counselor's tasks in helping the client. Labibah went to the second session not because she wanted to but rather, as she said, to "give it a chance." She felt turned off by the therapist's repetitions. She stopped the counseling sessions after her second visit. Labibah describes her reasoning as follows:

I just felt that after the first couple of sessions we were just talking about the same thing over and over, and if something was going to happen, she couldn't really make it happen by talking about it over and over. So I just thought this isn't really working.

This leads to another issue, namely, that some clients may desire quick solutions to their problems. Providing information to clients as to the strategy of treatment and what the client should expect lessens the client's anxiety and allows for cooperation.

Effective counselors must convey trustworthiness, especially to minority clients who enter the counseling relationship suspending trust until the person proves that he or she is worthy of trust (Cormier & Cormier, 1990).

Among the things that help establish trust is the counselor's ability to involve the client in the process of structuring the counseling relationship. Structuring refers to the interactional process between counselor and client, in which they arrive at similar perceptions of the role of the counselor, an understanding of what occurs in the counseling process, and an agreement on which outcome goals will be achieved (Brammer, Shostrom, & Abrego, 1989; Cormier & Cormier, 1990).

Counselor Is Disrespectful of the Client's Culture

Counselors may cause their clients to quit as a result of displaying a behavior that may be acceptable in the American culture while considered offensive in the culture of the client. For example, turning one's back to someone or extending one's feet to face another person are considered disrespectful in Arabic and Eastern cultures. Farida quit the session because, among other things, the counselor was placing her feet on the desk. Farida describes the situation, saying, "She was very dirty and she was sitting like this [Farida extends her feet and puts them up to illustrate the counselor's sitting] and her shoes were in my face. I said: I'm not going to put up with this. I'm not talking to her shoes."

It makes one wonder if such behavior is intentional or rather is a mere reflection of carelessness on behalf of the counselor. Even in Western cultures, the counselor is required to demonstrate warmth, attention, and positive regard for the client in his or her body language. Part of this is to lean forward toward the client to show closeness (Cormier & Cormier, 1991). Leaning backward, let alone extending the feet in the client's face, is a clear sign of distant, authoritarian, and cold feelings and attitudes and possibly disdain.

Farida was paying for her counseling sessions through the governmental medical coverage, Medicaid, for her son. This leads me to raise an important point, namely, the possibility of the existence of a direct link between the method of payment and the counselor's attitudes toward the client. My strong fear is that there might be a parallel between counselors' attitudes and those of public defendants appointed by courts who may show less concern or, at least, put forth less effort in defending their clients than privately paid lawyers. If this is true, I am forced to conclude that taxpayer money is being used to further traumatize the recipients of mental health care instead of helping them. Those who need help should be assigned quality care rather than treated as case numbers.

Counselor's Lack of Discretion

Part of genuineness involves the ability to be open, to share yourself, to self-disclose. Self-disclosure includes any information the counselor may convey or reveal to the client (Cormier & Cormier, 1991). Moderate self-disclosure is helpful and effective. Both low and high extremes of self-disclosure can prove counterproductive. While a low level may further the role distance between clients and counselors, a high level presents counselors as lacking discretion and as being untrustworthy (Cormier & Cormier, 1991). It is important for counselors not to disclose any information that compromises their competence and qualifications as capable therapists to deal with the issues that the client presents. Farida describes her counselor's self-disclosure, concluding that her counselor needs therapy herself. Farida states, "She told me that she was on Prozac and she was on a couple kinds of medicines herself and she had trouble dealing with issues. She was telling me that to feel more comfortable and I didn't mind it. I mean, it's okay; she's a human but no matter what her degree is in she's not going to be a help for me."

A real danger in overdisclosing is the risk of being perceived as needing therapy as much as the client. This could undermine the client's confidence in the counselor's ability to be helpful (Cormier & Cormier, 1991).

Counselor's Disability

Physical impairment that affects the counselor's ability to effectively communicate with the client has proven detrimental to the counseling relationship among Muslim clients. One more reason Farida stopped going to her counselor was because of the counselor's hearing impairment. She describes her experience as follows: "She couldn't hear very good and she wanted me to repeat things a hundred times and I didn't like that . . . no, but she has a hearing problem. Plus, I have an accent. She has a hearing problem and her office was where cars were going back and forth in the streets."

Counselor's Office Not Conveniently Located

In addition to the previously mentioned noise factor that affects counselor–client communication, safety and convenience of the office location are also important. Farida states, "And I didn't like going downtown."

This suggests that Muslim clients may prefer going to a counselor whose office is in close proximity or in an area that is easily accessible. This include such factors as safety, parking availability, and so on.

Counselor's Imposition of Own Values

In counselor–client interaction, it is impossible to be "value free." Values permeate every interaction, and counselors cannot be "scrupulously neutral" in their interaction with their clients (Corey, Corey, & Callanan, 1988; Cormier & Cormier, 1991). While attempting to minimize the influence of their values on clients, some counselors assume the role of world savior and confuse their religious missionary beliefs and attitudes with their ethical roles as helpers. After she separated from her Middle Eastern husband after 15 years of marriage and escaped without his knowledge from his country, Wahida became depressed and overwhelmed by having to raise her three daughters on her own without any financial support. Her therapist traumatized her even more. She describes the counselor's attempts to impose her values on her, saying, "She expressed that I should go to her church . . . she also used to tell me, 'No woman needs a man, especially in this society we don't need men. Many women raise children without a husband and without a father. You can do it—this is America.' It wasn't just a religious type of thing. It was more of a liberated woman's point of view."

After only three sessions, Wahida stopped seeing this counselor, and then had to deal with even more suffering and trauma.

In general, the fear of counseling that clients displayed as shown here was related, among other things, to a perceived invasiveness of the counselor, anticipated conflict over values (religious or cultural), and past unsuccessful experiences with other counselors.

ISSUES FOR COUNSELING AMERICAN MUSLIMS

From clients' participants, the issues that were involved in their counseling experience included eating disorders (the Hikmats' daughter), communication, and relations between family members (the Hikmats, Farida, and Pride's family); dealing with disability and/or death (Farida and

Pride); culture shock, children's custody, financial support, and restructuring a whole new life after divorce (Wahida); academic testing and value conflicts (the Palestinian family and their daughters); and children's rights versus responsibilities (Pride). The conflicts between continuing college education and religious values and between the child's choices and parents' expectations are also issues, as in the case of Labibah.

From the literature, it can be concluded that most issues, if not all, faced by ordinary Americans are increasingly becoming Muslims' issues. In an attempt to seek help, issues such as child abuse (sexual or otherwise), domestic violence (*Minaret*, March 1996), eating disorders (*Minaret*, July 1995), polygamy (*Minaret*, August 1996), matrimonial choice (*Minaret*, December 1995), self-control and expression of feelings (*Minaret*, March 1996), discrimination in schools and peer pressure (*Muslim Magazine*, January 1998), marital conflicts over financial issues (*Muslim Magazine*, April 1998), and singles' issues (particularly choosing a compatible mate) (*Minaret*, May 1996 and December 1995) are but a few examples of concerns expressed by Muslims to Muslim psychotherapists. The mere idea of having a corner in a publication for a psychotherapist to answer questions for fellow Muslim readers is an expression of the need for counseling.

By virtue of living in the U.S. context, Muslims are more likely than not to have more issues and concerns that are similar to those of the rest of Americans.

To best understand the dimension of such issues, factors that affect Muslim clients such as age, religion, and culture(s) must all be incorporated to determine the proper intervention, strategy, and techniques.

Personal- and Social-Related Issues

1. Adjustment in the new culture for new immigrants and refugees (culture-shock issues)
2. Children's identity in schools and in the social context of the United States
3. Child–parent and adolescent–parent relations (which often include rebellion)
4. Children's dating and the selection of a future profession and spouse
5. Changes in peer and family support systems
6. Caring for and dealing with aging or dying parents and relatives
7. Divorce, separation, or death of a spouse
8. Impotence regarding government and world problems, such as there being no national health care program, and the lack of ability to show support for fellow Muslims abroad. (In my own experience, I felt a tremendous need for counseling for Muslims over the 1990s and recent Gulf crisis, ethnic cleansing in both Bosnia and Kosovo, the high death rate among children of Iraq as a result of sanctions, and after September 11 and the subsequent invasions of Afghanistan and Iraq.)

9. Changes in family members because of acculturation, thus creating conflicts at home between needs and wants

Career-Related Issues

1. Employment, a critical issue, especially for new immigrants and refugees. This includes English language classes, standardized national exams, training, and job placement.

2. Religious issues in employment, such as not having the opportunity to participate in a congregation (Muslims' congregation is on Friday, which is a working day), participation in religious holidays and celebrations, or having to serve in a position that is seen as in contradiction to Islamic values (e.g., usury and liquor).

3. Termination from job, be it voluntary (quitting or retiring) or involuntary (being fired or forced to retire). Involuntary termination may be due to adherence to Islamic values, such as women insisting on wearing their traditional Islamic dress.

4. Job dissatisfaction.

5. Career culmination or demotion; lack of a challenge; realization of unfulfillment; burnout; feeling trapped.

6. Career obsolescence. This may be very evident in immigrants who come after serving as distinguished medical doctors, engineers, teachers, and college professors but feel unable to find similar jobs here because of language or other barriers and then resort to low-paying jobs in fast-food restaurants, gas stations, and so on. To illustrate this point, an experienced attorney from Bosnia who speaks English fluently was hired as a translator for the refugee center, but after some time, he left the job to work as a paralegal. He felt overwhelmed and disappointed that he could not satisfy the requirements to work as a lawyer.

7. Limited upward mobility.

8. Desire for more leisure or decreased career stamina.

9. Changing work or life values (e.g., women becoming more assertive).

10. Technological changes.

11. Desire for continuing education.

12. Conflict between religious values and the need for a job (e.g., liquor-, gambling-, and pork-related jobs for Muslims).

Physical-Related Issues

1. Physical changes (gradual or trauma/disease)

2. Health emergencies

3. Reconciling personal and public image of physical self

Other Issues

1. Interfaith and intercultural marriages
2. Emotional and mental changes
3. Financial emergencies and pressures
4. Relocation
5. Retirement planning

New converts are often faced with resistance, opposition, and even rejection from their immediate family members. Leaving such issues unexamined may lead to dissent, anger, and rebellion against societal and familial lack of support. Many new Muslims often ask, Why am I allowed to choose the next president of the United States but not allowed to choose my own religion?

Future research will be helpful in determining the specific issues that concern Muslims and the best way of dealing with them.

Table 5.1 shows a comparison between the different counseling models—pastoral, educational, and medical—with recommendations as to which can work best with issues faced by Muslims. Table 5.2 compares different counseling approaches and what issues each can be best effective in dealing with.

Table 5.1
A Comparison between Different Counseling Models and Their Effectiveness: Cases with Muslim Clients

The counseling model	Issues that work best with Muslims	Counselor's characteristics
Pastoral counseling	Grief, death, natural disasters, illness, tragedies, etc. All issues related to or connected with faith and religion. This model works well with refugees who left their countries as a result of natural disasters or civil wars or who lost loved ones in wars.	This approach requires the counselor to be a Muslim. If the counselor is not a Muslim, Muslim clients may be skeptical and unaccepting.
Educational counseling	Communication within family, career counseling, skill development, budgeting, parenting, husband-wife relations, etc.	Same sex counselors. If male clients are assigned female counselors, they may show resistance and eventually withdraw.
Medical Counseling	Any condition caused by chemical imbalance or requiring medications such as depression, anxiety, obsessive compulsive disorder, etc.	Counselors need to be highly trustworthy to keep the client's confidence. Most Muslim clients do not prefer a Muslim counselor, psychologist or psychiatrist for the fear of losing confidentiality.

Table 5.2
Counseling Approaches and Their Use with Muslim Clients

The Counseling Approach	Recommended for	Not helpful for
Psychoanalytical	Uncovering old conflicts, fears, anxieties and other deeply rooted problems.	Family dynamics for the fear of breaking family ties and putting members against each other. It is also objectionable due to the fact that it suggests that some problems are beyond the person's control, which is against the religious teachings.
Adlerian	Social and community relations; rehabilitation from domestic abuse, racism, and victimization; family relations; and communication within family.	Religious-based or related issues, such as grief, loss, and natural disasters.
Person-centered	Client-community relations, political activism, career advancement, and communication with one's own peers or superiors.	Parent-child relations in particular and family relations in general.
Behavior	Education, training, eating disorders, budgeting, and family relations from Muslims' perspective. This model may work mostly with immigrants who are looking for a guide, a teacher, and an instructor.	Private and intimate issues, such as the husband/wife relationship and issues of a religious nature.
Existential	None	All
Gestalt	Immediate and practical needs of clients, including family issues, refugees, and communication using body language and gestures.	Intimate relations where Muslim clients feel most reserved and unable to express their intimate feelings.
Transactional	Educated Muslim clients who can benefit from the contract and the power it gives to the client.	Low-educated clients and clients in crisis.
Rational-emotive and cognitive-behavioral therapy	None, for the fear it creates conflict between the client and the counselor, thus leading to a withdrawal from counseling.	All.
Reality therapy	Issues related to various systems allowing Muslim clients to deal with assimilation and acculturation.	Social injustice and inequality, racism and discrimination.

CHAPTER 6

Summary and Conclusion

REVIEW

This book raises the question, what is the status of American Muslims with regard to counseling and the mental health professions? There is no doubt that the American Muslim population aspires for inclusion, understanding, and respect in society, including the mental health field.

Many health professionals, both physical and mental, are seeking to understand the particular faith traditions of their clients in order to sensitively and effectively serve them. While understanding is required for all clients, it is more so for Muslims, especially after the terrorist attacks of September 11, 2001. In addition to the documented widespread misunderstanding of Islam in the media and education, hate crimes, prejudice, and discrimination are increasing particularly after these tragic events.

Most current educational and training programs do not give much attention to the inclusion of minority populations (Ibrahim, 1991; Pedersen, 1991; Sue, 1989). It is encouraging, however, to know that awareness of religious diversity is on the rise, and such an awareness must be included as one of the requirements for adequate multicultural competencies by mental health professional organizations.

By explaining the various aspects of counseling and therapy through the experiences of both Muslim clients and of professionals, this book helps ordinary Muslims develop informed opinions about counseling. They will be able to know whether and when they might seek counseling as well as what issues could be helped by that counseling. Thus, they would know what to expect.

An important feature of this book is that it allows Muslim clients to voice their concerns and tell their experiences. Through the approach of symbolic interaction, I provide the opportunity for Muslim clients to articulate their constructed meanings for themselves and for others, their needs and expectations, their hopes and fears, and their painful experiences and successful outcomes.

On the other hand, this book familiarizes counselors and therapists with the Islamic religion and Muslim cultures. Furthermore, it explains the factors that influence Muslims' identity formation, including sources and the forms of stereotypes and prejudices in society that work against the American Muslim population. Finally, it points out to professionals the severe deficiency of research and publications on American Muslims as part of the sources of incompetence in dealing with Muslim clients.

Despite the long history of Muslims' presence in the United States, the remarkable increase in their numbers as well as institutions, and their visibility within their communities from the inner cities to the suburbs across the country, they remain almost unknown, much less accommodated, particularly in the field of counseling.

Information about Islam and Muslims, if present, is biased, distorted, and shaped to foster fear, contempt, and even hatred toward Muslims. While education about Muslims and their needs in the field of mental health is essential, it is not expected by itself to result in an immediate improvement of the perception of or in increased sensitivity toward them. In fact, research shows that education does not always eradicate prejudice. Many educated people hide their prejudice by espousing the liberal values and beliefs of the dominant culture while doing very little to change matters (Jackman & Muha, 1984). Alterab (1997), who studied attitudes toward Muslims, concludes that "it may be that educated people tend to mask their attitudes through 'political correctness'" (p. 120).

This fact does not undermine the need for education on Islam and Muslims for counseling professionals who are interested in becoming competent in dealing with their Muslim clients. If anything, it makes education all the more important. Without it, breakthroughs would be impossible. This is, in fact, what this book does; that is, it creates a path for progress in counseling by including American Muslims through the sharing of actual interaction information.

IMPLICATIONS FOR COUNSELORS

American Muslims, whether immigrants or indigenous, are constantly negotiating the meaning of being Muslims in America. The debate and its outcome are based mainly on the issue of identity. On the one hand, identity is made complex by the socioeconomic and political factors that significantly impact the various aspects of clients' lives. On the other hand, it is made even more complex by the difficulty to reconcile American cultural practices, public negative misrepresentations of Islam and Muslims, and U.S. foreign policies, to mention only a few examples, with what most Muslims perceive as requirements of an Islamic identity. Such conflicts of identity have resulted in the development of two major groups among American Muslims. The first group is characterized by the belief in the impossibility of reconciling being an American with being a Muslim. Members of this group have, therefore, resorted to either withdrawal or assimilation. While the first of these two subgroups deserted society to live in uninhabited areas of the United States and, therefore, are called "isolationists," the latter resorted to full assimilation in society to avoid being viewed as "different."

The second group seeks to balance the two and live as good Muslims in America. Members of this group, comprising the largest number of American Muslims, are struggling to practice their religion and, at the same time, participate as full citizens in American society. They are faced with the question of identity on a daily basis at schools, at workplaces, in social activities, and in neighborhoods. This challenge is further complicated by individuals' concerns for their public image within the Muslim community as well as society at large. This simply means that individuals are often forced to make the difficult decision of choosing one of the two. In many instances, acceptance in one group means rejection by the other. The issue of identity and resolving the conflicts related to that identity must, therefore, take a priority on the counselor's list of issues. Ponterotto et al. (1995) recommend that counselors

- understand the socioeconomic and political factors that significantly impact the psychosocial, political, and economic development of ethnic and culturally diverse group;
- help clients to understand/maintain/resolve their own sociocultural identification; and
- understand the intention of culture, gender, sexual orientation on behavior and needs. (p. 610)

Identity development models identified with other cultural and religious minorities may be used as a guide for a possible parallel between Muslims and other minority groups in this regard, but one should never attempt to forcibly apply them on Muslim clients, which might cause more harm than good.

Because of the wide diversity among Muslims both religiously and culturally, an understanding of both religious and cultural affiliation and preferences of each individual client becomes an essential element to any meaningful counseling relationship.

Since the majority of American Muslims are immigrants who come from cultures that embody traditional forms of support systems and counseling, this book does not attempt to replace such clients' existing traditional support systems with counseling. To the contrary, it encourages counselors and therapists to take into account and consider taking advantage of effective and acceptable means of guidance and support systems that may be available within the cultures of their Muslim clients. Furthermore, it draws the attention of counselors to the societal and organizational resources available that can provide more understanding as to the specific issues that counselors may face with Muslim clients.

The information presented serves a dual purpose. First, it helps explain the sources of negative attitudes of counselors toward their Muslim clients that may manifest in biased assessment and diagnosis, mistreatment in the counseling sessions, and early termination. Second, it explains the attitudes and perceptions of Muslim clients to both the counseling process and counselors.

Muslims' perception of counseling and therapy is influenced by both religious and cultural influences. The fact that Islam is seen by Muslims as a total way of life leads most Muslims to identify themselves as religious, and religious Muslim individuals to see every issue as religious, so that a resolution to that issue cannot be achieved without involving religion. Such individuals may seek the help of a religious authority rather than go to a counselor.

Because of the widespread confusion of religious teachings with cultures in the minds of many Muslims, cultural issues may be seen as religious. To those individuals, the religious affiliation of the counselor is very important. It may be tempting to generalize that Muslim clients prefer seeing Muslim counselors. Surprisingly, many Muslim clients may prefer non-Muslim counselors. Some of the reasons cited by clients include being embarrassed by discussing personal issues with someone who attends the same mosque, and that the counselor's children may go to the same school as that of the client or the client's children, in turn compromising their confidentiality and being a constant reminder of the concerns they wanted to get over. Other participants expressed the view that the counselor does not need to be a Muslim or familiar with Islamic teachings unless the problem is religious in nature. I, therefore, conclude that the preference of Muslim clients for Muslim counselors depends on the following factors:

(a) The client's religiosity. The more the client identifies with religion, the more likely he or she would prefer a Muslim counselor. Furthermore, the religiosity of the counselor would also be a factor.

(b) The client's perception of the issue at hand. If the client perceives the problem to be religious or religiously based, he or she is more likely to seek a solution from a religious authority where the solution is based on religious teachings.

(c) The location of the office of the Muslim counselor. Muslim clients may be deterred from seeking counseling by a Muslim counselor if the counselor's office is located in or near a Muslim's place of worship or the Muslim's public institution (e.g., a school, a social service agency, a mosque, a community center, and so on). The reason for this, as participants expressed it, is the likelihood of being seen there by someone they know.

(d) The size of the community in which the client and counselor exist. The larger the city is, the larger the number of Muslims there will be. This means that the Muslim counselor is not likely to know all or even most of the Muslims in that area, in turn minimizing the Muslim client's fear with respect to compromising confidentiality. It also reduces the risk of being seen at the office by other Muslims who know, or are known to, the client.

With constantly changing roles of imams coupled with the fact that many Muslim individuals and families may seek the imam's help for emotional, psychological, and mental concerns that require education, training, and expertise beyond those of most imams, imams need to understand their limitations and seek the education and training necessary to enable them to separate between religious education and counseling. Furthermore, they need to direct their clients to seek help from their medical or mental health professionals.

Competent counselors must, therefore, evaluate the client's concept of religiosity as well as the client's perception of the problem. The result of the evaluation will help determine whether religion needs to be incorporated in the counseling procedures and techniques and to what level.

Speaking of cultural factors, since the American Muslim population is made up of widely diverse groups, not all of them have the same perception of counseling and therapy. Among participants, I found only two groups who have developed positive perceptions of counseling. These two groups are white American Muslims and Muslims who have had positive counseling experiences.

Other groups include African American Muslims and immigrants. They were found to have negative perceptions of counseling for a variety of reasons. While African American Muslims feel underrepresented and underserved, most immigrant Muslims are unaware of the existence, let alone the procedures and outcome, of such services.

After counseling became known to them, they did not seek it for one or more of the following reasons:

- Equating counseling with craziness
- Viewing counseling as a threat to one's own authority, autonomy, or status
- Seeing counseling as an expression of lacking family, friends, and supportive relatives
- Lack of awareness of the procedures and expected outcome of counseling

- Lack of education in American higher-education institutions, acculturation, or assimilation
- Suspicions about the counselor's values and feelings toward Islam and Muslims due to differences in religion, political views, and historic and contemporary conflicts (e.g., the Arab–Israeli conflict in the Middle East)
- Fear of the unknown and worries about overwhelming financial liability

Acculturation is an obvious fact of the positive acceptance of counseling. By "acculturation," I mean the level of identifying with the attitudes, lifestyles, and values of the dominant culture. Because it is an evolutionary process, the two most important factors found to be accelerating the process of acculturation are education in American higher-education institutions and long residence in the United States. Long residence, however, is considered a factor in speeding the acculturation process only when the person is not limiting his or her social activities or employment to ethnic, national, or religious acquaintances.

There is also the matter of the degree of satisfaction with prior counseling encounters. Muslims who had experiences in counseling reported that the most important factor in their decisions with respect to whether to continue or stop counseling was their experience in the first counseling session. Muslim individuals with positive experiences continued their participation to the end and said that they would recommend counseling to others when they need it. Others whose experiences with counselors were negative or not encouraging either changed the counselor or quit counseling altogether.

SPECIFIC RECOMMENDATIONS FOR COUNSELORS

The diversity of American Muslims constitutes a great challenge to the counseling profession. Each local Muslim community, for instance, has a different mix of Muslims from various ethnic backgrounds and of different generations. As a result of this cultural meeting, there is always the risk of a "clash of cultures" or a "clash of civilizations." Some cultural practices, such as female genital mutilation, child beating, spousal abuse, and forcing young children (particularly girls) into marriage, require only common sense to be regarded dangerous, wrong, and indefensible. Furthermore, they are illegal in both Islamic and American law. In such cases, counselors are asked neither to ignore their conscientious objections nor to fail their moral responsibilities and legal obligations. These problems tend to be reduced, if not eliminated, with the process of integration and acculturation. Counselors' awareness of the possibility of the existence of such practices must warrant preventive approaches, including education about the pros and cons (psychological, social, and legal) through individual as well as group counseling.

To overcome religious and cultural factors that do not amount to the violation of universal human rights and the constitutional or legal rights of individuals (including minors), yet that do hinder the effectiveness of counseling and therapy, my recommendations to counselors are as follows:

- Evaluate the client's religiosity.
- Assess the client's understanding of the nature of the problem.
- Examine the client's perception of mental health.
- Collaborate with experts from local and (if needed) national Islamic organizations in conducting seminars and workshops to inform Muslims about the professions and their procedures and advantages. Financial liabilities and charges must also be explained.
- Team up with Muslim physicians in local areas in order for them to refer their Muslim patients when needed. Chances are that such referrals will carry more weight because Muslim patients are likely to trust Muslim physicians' professional judgment.
- Network with Muslim social service agencies in order for them to include you on their lists of providers.
- Counsel Muslim clients from their own perspectives rather than from your own.
- Try to employ traditional means of support systems that are available in the cultural and/or religious community of the client.
- Develop a positive impression and rapport with your clients from the very beginning of the counseling relationship.

RECOMMENDATIONS FOR THE COUNSELING PROFESSION

Since counseling is the product of Western culture and thought, many of its basic assumptions reflect the social, economic, and political context of Western Euro-American cultures. Most counselors themselves are also the products of these very cultures. In addition to the fact that such assumptions tend to be exclusive of minority groups, they are more so for Muslims because of the widespread negative perceptions of Islam and Muslims in American culture and institutions.

The counseling profession has been regarded as a helping profession and, therefore, is required to provide for the individual's optimum development and well-being. Since individuals exist and function in social contexts, not in isolation, counseling must include these factors in the understanding of human needs and aspirations. The client's religious perspective is yet another factor that is often ignored by counselors despite the fact that it is an essential element of human development. For Muslims, the factors of religion and social context are crucial for successful multicultural counseling.

In addition to the pressures Muslims face in counseling, educational, social, economic, and political systems are at work in the acceleration of the process of their acculturation and Americanization. This may be considered helpful even when it is not, but, in fact, it can be harmful and even destructive. Crollius (1984) states,

The experiences of our history make us painfully aware of the fact that not all contact between different cultures means automatically an enrichment for the cultures concerned. Culture-contact can also be destructive. Our world knows many groups of people who live in a state of "cultural schizophrenia," becoming gradually alienated from their own culture without finding a home in the culture that pretends to absorb them. Every one-directional process of cultural assimilation ignores the riches of originality and creativity in a given culture and leads to an impoverishment of human values. A fruitful communication between cultures has to take on the form of a dialogue (p. 50)

Because the acculturation process is likely to be forced on newcomers rather than produced through constructive dialogue, it often creates a feeling of resentment toward society's norms and a state of helplessness, leading to possible withdrawal from society and its institutions.

While I do not expect that multicultural education alone will eradicate prejudice in counseling, it is nevertheless an essential element for the counselors' competence. It was not until the 1980s that the idea of multiculturalism began its unprecedented growth. This means that older generations of counselors have missed the opportunity to receive the education and training necessary for satisfactory performance with minority clients. Recent graduates, as represented by one of the two counselors I interviewed, have received multicultural education and training but often not in relation to Muslims. Unfortunately, in her case, while textbooks assigned to the class included at least some material on Muslims, the professor dismissed it as not important or nonexistent.

Multicultural education should, therefore, begin in the early stages to protect against the influences of racism and prejudice that are prevalent with respect to Muslims. This education must be aimed at familiarizing students with the Islamic religion and the vast range of diversity in Islamic cultures. It must also include the history and demography of Muslims' presence in the United States.

Counselor education programs should stipulate multicultural education and training as requirements for graduation in all counseling specializations. American society is so diverse that such diversity is felt in all facets of life. More specifically, educational and training programs for counselors should focus on the issues and needs of American Muslims.

Counselors in schools are overwhelmed with the number of students they have to help. As a result, individual counseling is a luxury to most students and most counselors (Boutwell & Myrick, 1992). The quality of counseling services must be given a priority over the quantity of cases brought to a conclusion.

The Muslim client–counselor relationship is not limited to voluntary office visitations for normal life issues. Rather, it extends to include sudden and unexpected tragedies that indiscriminately affect all people living in the particular area, such as hurricanes, floods, random violence, and plane crashes. This necessitates the inclusion of Muslims in both the educational and the training aspects of multicultural counseling programs. Furthermore, multicultural competency must warrant the requirement of adequate education and training specific to a minority group before working with members of that group. Such specialization should be made equivalent to the specialization in issues of counseling, such as family, group, and career counseling. This specialization should also be made a requirement for licensing and accreditation. To specialize in the counseling of a particular minority group, one must be familiar with the group's history, demography, challenges, and needs.

Examining the widely publicized and widely accepted model of multicultural counseling competencies by Sue, Arredondo, and McDavis (1992), three main characteristics have been determined as standards for multicultural competencies: (a) the counselor's awareness of his or her own assumptions, values, and biases; (b) understanding the worldview of the culturally different client; and (c) developing appropriate intervention strategies and techniques.

For other minority groups, according to Sue et al. (1992), "A body of literature exists documenting the widespread ineffectiveness of traditional counseling approaches and techniques when applied to racial and ethnic minority populations" (p. 627).

For American Muslims, the situation is even worse because all the previously mentioned standards are lacking in counselors, counseling programs, and society as a whole with respect to Muslim clients.

D'Andrea and Daniels (1995) recommend "establishing the principles of multicultural counseling as the centerpiece of the ethical standards of counseling profession" (p. 31). This model (as well as others) fails to address elements such as the importance of religion and biases in standardized assessment and testing as essential components in multicultural counseling. Furthermore, this model fails to encourage counselors to utilize traditional forms of support and counseling that may have roots in the cultures of minority clients.

In addition to the requirement of adequate education and training for accreditation, Ms. Field, one of the counselor participants in this book, suggests that such training be done more constantly and at regular intervals.

If education and training programs were to include American Muslims, the first obstacle they would face is the lack of sufficient research and studies done among this population.

Psychological testing needs more attention and complete reform. Bias in testing leads counselors to label Muslim clients as disabled, resistant, incompetent, deviant, abnormal, or any other label of inadequacy and incompatibility. Testing includes defining the problem, gathering and understanding information, and coping with the problem.

Thus, in their attempt to organize, interpret, and understand person–environment relations within any theoretical perspective of the many theories of development, counselors are likely to err because of the following:

(a) Lack of understanding the client's frame of reference.
(b) Inherent biases that exist in standardized testing and that often lead to discrimination. Test biases occur in one or more of three areas: content, internal structure, and selection.

The combination of a lack of understanding and testing bias is devastating. The two young girls were victimized and labeled as disabled. Such a label, had it remained, would have stayed with them for the rest of their lives. It becomes necessary, therefore, to modify testing batteries and procedures to accommodate the general cultures, subcultures, and even countercultures of Muslims.

Counselors need to be competent in using the psychological approach relevant to and appropriate for the particular situation of their clients. For instance, immigrant Muslims may struggle to deal with issues related to integration to American culture, including learning the language, searching for jobs, and advancing their skills to match the job market's demands. They may also need to deal with issues of discrimination at schools and places of employment.

In such cases, the use of the psychoanalytical approach, which focuses on the past as a major determinant of the present, would not be very helpful. On the one hand, this is likely to trigger the client's resistance because it tends to compromise one's loyalty to family and culture; on the other hand, it may not be sufficiently practical or expedient to help clients in a time of economic distress. Problems also tend to have recent sources of causation. For instance, most recent immigrants are Muslims who fled their homelands because of violent conflicts and wars, such as in the case of Somalia, Bosnia, and Kosovo. Large numbers of these immigrants are professionals, including medical doctors, lawyers, engineers, and so on. Despite the high level of education, long experience, and prestigious status they had back home, they are told that they are neither adequately prepared nor legally allowed to practice their professions in the United States. This further exacerbates trauma and intensifies feelings of helplessness. Counselors need to handle all these matters with a great deal of sensitivity and expediency by using the appropriate approaches and techniques.

An African American Muslim woman, for instance, can be subjected to multiple forms of discrimination because of race, gender, and religion, a syndrome that is referred to in the literature as "multiple oppression" (Jackson, 1991). Several cases made the headlines because qualified Muslim women were denied jobs or services just because of their Islamic dress. One incident reflects both the misunderstanding of Islam and discrimination against Muslims, as reported by the *Arizona Republic* newspaper (January 20, 2000) under the title "Bus Trip Turns into Bias Issue: Greyhound Driver Left Two Muslim Women at Stop." Mark Shaffer of the newspaper wrote, "First, the African-American woman in Islamic dress was left behind with her elderly mother by a Greyhound driver who pulled away early from a rest stop on the Navajo Nation. Then, when the pair finally caught up with the bus in Flagstaff, she said the driver told her if she had a problem with the treatment, 'Go tell it to [Louis] Farrakhan.'" In such cases, the counselor must be understanding of civil right issues as well as of the daily struggle of minority groups to gain equality.

Dealing with white and black American Muslim converts may entail working on issues related to family relationships. It is not unusual that after converting to Islam a person is disowned and deserted by dearly beloved family members. This situation is likely to further feelings of alienation and isolation already at work in society at large.

Seeing counseling through the eyes of Muslim clients is an important theme of this book. It helps us familiarize ourselves with the needs of Muslim clients in counseling.

It is very hard for many Muslim individuals to initiate the request for counseling. Unless the person is familiar with counseling, the decision to use counseling is likely to come from someone else, usually a male authority in the family (e.g., a father or a husband), a community authority (e.g., a judge, a school's principal, or an employer), or a social or health professional (e.g., a social worker or a medical doctor). Women agree to seek counseling only when they feel at risk and realize that their lives will be difficult if they do not. In general, Muslim clients need to be pushed by someone other than themselves to go to counseling.

Some of the factors that influence the counseling relationship are gender, religion, and political affiliation. As for gender, counselors need to realize that Muslims in general observe strict rules regulating the relationship between the sexes. Men and women usually do not mix, shake hands, keep eye contact, sit in close proximity to each other, or exchange physical contact through touching, hugging, and so on.

It would, therefore, be helpful if Muslim clients were referred to a counselor of the same sex. It would be even more accommodating to discuss this issue with the client before making the referral. During counseling sessions, counselors should not assume that Western values are universal and attempt eye contact or physical touching to show affection or sympathy. If the client is of the opposite sex, it is advisable that the counselor keep the door open unless requested by the client. On some occasions and for cultural reasons, a male Muslim client may not want to receive counseling from a woman, for it would be viewed as an insult to his manhood.

Although the issue of religion was discussed earlier, I would add that counselors should refrain from passing judgment on Muslim women as oppressed just because they cover their heads and wear long clothes.

Muslims whose original culture has been involved in political or military conflicts with another group may likely resent going to a counselor from that group, such as an Arab (particularly a Palestinian) seeing a Jewish counselor, a Bosnian or Kosovar seeing a Serbian counselor, or a Pakistani seeing an Indian counselor. This should not be interpreted that the client's stereotypes are valid or appropriate. Rather, it means that counselors may need to make additional efforts to assure their clients of their competency and neutrality.

Muslims regard counseling as good and helpful when the counselor demonstrates positive regard, displays interest in the client, and respects the culture as well as the religion of the client. Muslims develop favorable impressions when counselors are not judgmental. When a counselor starts stereotyping, individual or group clients may quit counseling. The counselor also needs to show humility by acknowledging limitations and asking questions about the culture and values of the client. The notion of experience may vary from one client to another. Muslim clients also prefer experienced counselors.

Muslims' views of bad counseling includes the opposites of the components of good counseling. Furthermore, they add other elements that would prevent them from seeking counseling with such counselors. One of these elements is the appearance of the counselor, which may be trendy and fashionable but not perceived as such by Muslims (e.g., men wearing earrings or dressing casually). To overcome these cultural differences, counselors may find it helpful to discuss with clients how they feel about theses issues and consequently inform them that they are personal choices and that they will not affect the counseling relationship.

The convenience and safety of the counselor's office location would also encourage Muslim clients to seek counseling.

This book is but a step in the long and rough road ahead. The road is to understanding and accommodating American Muslims in mental health fields. Further research and studies are required and indeed overdue. The task is equally challenging to both scholars and researchers on the one hand and the Muslim population on the other. For researchers, the challenge is how to guard against their biases in attempting to reach out to the Muslim population, in establishing rapport that allows reliable and valid conclusions, and in examining the pressing issues that concern the Muslim population. For Muslims, the challenge is how to open up to the new realities of living in American society, thus allowing research and service to be provided to them with the help and support they deserve and frequently need.

By putting this work before my fellow Muslims and my colleagues in the counseling profession, I hope I have initiated the charge, broken the barrier, and opened the door for a promising combination of scholarship and services.

Glossary

A'lims: A scholar in Islamic jurisprudence and theology.

Allah: The one God who created all of creation and sent all messengers.

Athan or Adhan: The call to prayers.

Burku', Burda, or Niqab: Face cover worn by women from various cultures, including but not limited to Muslims.

Eidul Adha: The festival of sacrifice. It is celebrated on the tenth of the twelfth month of the Islamic lunar calendar, recognizing the culmination of the *hajj* rites at Mecca and, at the same time, commemorating the attempt of the Prophet Abraham to sacrifice his son Ishmail.

Eidul-Fitr: The celebration that marks the end of the month of Ramadan.

Fitra: Pure natural instinct or pure Islamic faith.

Hajj: Pilgrimage to Mecca. It is required once in a lifetime for every adult Muslim male or female who is financially and physically able.

Hijab: A Muslim woman's head cover.

Hijra (Hegira): The migration of the Prophet Muhammad from Mecca to Medina, marking the beginning of the Islamic lunar calendar, which is usually 11 days shorter then the common-era year.

Ibadat: Acts of worship.

Jihad: Struggling in all aspects of life, including combating. It can be classified into minor and major jihad. While the minor jihad refers to combating, the major one refers to struggling against one's own self and temptations.

Koran (Qur'an): The holy scripture of Islam. To Muslims, it is the final revelation from God to Muhammad. It includes ethical, moral, and legal codes and is considered the first source of legislation in Islam.

Kuhulah: Over 40 years old.

Mahd: Cradle.

Masajid (pl. of Masjid): Mosque. Muslims' place of worship.

Ma˙zun: A marriage-officiating officer in the Muslim world.

Mua˙malat: Customs, transactions, and human relations.

Muhammad: The Messenger of Islam, who was born in 570 c.e. in Mecca, Arabia, and who died in 622 c.e. in Medina, Arabia.

Niqab: Face cover worn by women from Arab cultures, particularly Muslim women.

Qadi: The Arabic word for "judge."

Radaa˙: Breast feeding.

Ramadan: The month of fasting for Muslims.

Salat: Prayers.

Sawm: Fasting. One of the five pillars of Islam for Muslims to abstain from foods, drink, and sensual pleasure during the month of Ramadan (the ninth month in the Islamic lunar calendar).

Shabab: Stage of youth.

Shahadah: Testimony of faith summarized in the utterance of the following statement: "I bear witness that there is no god but God and that Muhammad is the Messenger of God." It is necessary for someone to say this in order to be admitted to the religion of Islam and to the community of Muslims.

Ummah: The world community of Muslims.

Zakat: Charity. Muslims are obligated, if they reach certain financial status, to give annual charity to the poor.

Bibliography

References

Abu-Lughod. (1990). Anthropology's orient: The boundaries of theory on the Arab world. In H. Sharabi (Ed.), *Theory, politics, and the Arab world* (pp. 81–131). New York: Routledge.

Abudabbeh, N. (1996). Arab families. In M. McGoldrick, J. Giordano, & J. Pearce (Eds.), *Ethnicity and family therapy* (pp. 333–346). New York: Guilford Press.

Ahmed, G. M. (1991). Muslim organizations in the United States. In Y. Haddad (Ed.), *The Muslims in America* (pp. 11–24). New York: Oxford University Press.

Al-Ahsan, A. (1992). *Ummah or nation? Identity crisis in contemporary Muslim society.* London: Islamic Foundation.

Al-Faruqi, L. (1988). *Women, Muslim society, and Islam.* American Trust Publications.

Al-Faruqi, L. (1995). *Muslim women and Islamic societies.* Indianapolis: Amana Publications.

Almanac. (1992). (45th ed.) Boston: Houghton Mifflin.

Almeida, R. (1996). Hindu, Christian, and Muslim families. In M. McGoldrick, J. Giordano, & J. Pearce (Eds.), *Ethnicity and family therapy* (pp. 395–423). New York: Guilford Press.

Altareb, B. (1996, October). Islamic spirituality in America: A middle path to unity. *Counseling and Values, 41*, 29–38.

Altareb, B. (1997). *Attitudes towards Muslims: Initial scale development.* Unpublished doctoral diss., Ball State University.

American Muslim Council (1992). *The Muslim population in the United States: A brief statement.* Washington, DC: AMC.

At-Tall, S. (1990). Stages of human development and their educational needs (in Arabic). In F. Malkawy (Ed.), *Papers of Educational Conference, Vol. 1: Towards building a contemporary educational theory* (in Arabic) (pp. 327–357). Amman, Jordan: The International Institute of Islamic Thought (IIIT) and Yarmuk University.

Atkinson, D. R., Morten, G., & Sue, D. W. (1979). *Counseling American minorities: A cross cultural perspective.* Dubuque, IA: Wm C Brown.

Ba-Yunus, I., & Siddiqui, M. (1998). *A report on Muslim population in the United States.* New York: CAMRI.

Badri, Malik. (1979). *The dilemma of Muslim psychologists.* London: MWH London Publishers.

Bagby, I. (Ed.). (1994). *Muslim resource guide.* Fountain Valley, CA: Islamic Resource Institute.

Becker, H., & Geer, B. (1958). Participant observation and interviewing: A comparison. *Human Organization, 16,* 28–32.

Bekkum, H. J. (1994). *Adolescence and ethnicity: International journey of adolescent youth* (Vol. 4). U.K.: Academic Publishers.

Bennoune, K. (1995). Islamic fundamentalism represses women. In D. Bender & B. Leone (Eds.), *Islam: Opposing viewpoints* (pp. 64–71). San Diego, CA: Green Haven Press.

Bergin, A. (1980). Psychotherapy and religious values. *Journal of Counseling and Clinical Psychology, 48*(1), 11–13.

Bernstein, R. (1993, 2 May). Muslims in America: From slave trade to 60's explosion. *New York Times,* p. A1.

Bhatt, A. (1994, 3 February). Speaker attacks media portrayal of Islam. *The Daily Orange,* p. 1.

Bogdan, R., & Biklen, S. (1992). *Qualitative research for education.* Boston: Allyn & Bacon.

Boutwell, D., & Myrick, R. (1992). The go for it club. *Elementary School Guidance and Counseling, 27*(1), 65–72.

Brammer, L. M., Shostrom, E. L., & Abrego, P. J. (1989). *Therapeutic psychology: Fundamentals of counseling and psychotherapy* (5th ed.). Englewood Cliffs, NJ: Prentice Hall.

Brumberg, J. (1989). *Fasting girls: The history of anorexia nervosa.* Ontario, Canada: Penguin Book Academy.

Buckley, W. (1993, 8 July). U.S. culture and fundamentalist Islam don't mix. *The Post Standard,* p. A8.

Burke, M. T. (1998, winter). From the chair: The CACREP connection. In Miller, Summit results in information of spirituality competencies. *Journal of Counseling and Development, 71*(4), 498–502.

Cantor, N., & Mischel, W. (1979). Prototypicality and personality effects on free recall and personality impressions. *Journal of Research in Personality, 13*(2), 330–342.

Carter, R., & El-Hindi, A. (n.d.). Understanding the issues faced by Islamic families: A study to inform school counselors and teachers. Unpublished minigrant proposal, Texas Tech University, College of Education.

Combs, A. W. (1986). What makes a good helper? A person-centered approach. *Person-Centered Review, 1,* 51–61.

Constantine, M. (1999). Racism's impact on counselor's professional and personal lives: A response to the personal narratives on racism. *Journal of Counseling and Development: Special Issue, Racism: Healing Its Effects, 77*(1), 68–72.

Cooper, M. H. (1993, 30 April). Muslims in America: Can they find place in society? *New York Times*, p. A1.

Corey, G. (1991). *Case approach to counseling and psychotherapy* (3rd ed.). Pacific Grove, CA: Brooks/Cole.

Corey, G., Corey, M., & Callanan, B. (1988). *Professional and ethical issues in counseling and psychotherapy* (3rd ed.). Pacific Grove, CA: Brooks/Cole.

Cormier & Cormier. (1991). *Interviewing strategies for helpers: Fundamental skills and cognitive behavioral interventions.* (3rd edition). Pacific Grove, CA: Brooks/Cole.

Cornell, G. (1990, 13 October). Moslems seek new acceptance: A religion of American life. *Syracuse Herald Journal*, p. A12.

Council on American-Islamic Relations (CAIR). (1997). *An employer's guide to Islamic religious practices* (2nd ed.). Washington, DC: CAIR.

Crollius, A. (1984). Inculturation and the meaning of culture. In A. Crollius & S. Nekeramihigo (Eds.), *What is so new about inculturation? Inculturation: Working papers on living faith and culture* (pp. 33–54). Rome: Cultures and Religions Center, Pontifical Gregorian University.

Cross, W. E. (1971). The negro-to-black conversion experience. *Black World, 20*, 12–27.

D'Andrea, M., & Daniels, J. (1995). Helping students learn to get along: Assessing the effectiveness of a multicultural developmental guidance project. *Elementary School Guidance and Counseling: Special Issue, Developmental Issues, 30*(2), 143–154.

Deane, F., & Chamberlain, K. (1994). Treatment fearfulness and distress as predictors of professional psychological help-seeking. *British Journal of Guidance and Counseling, 22*(2), 207–217.

Denny, F. (1995). *Islam.* San Francisco: Harper.

Docherty, J. (1997). Barriers to the diagnosis of depression in primary care. *Journal of Clinical Psychology, 58*(supplement 1), 5–10.

Draguns, J. (1989). Dilemmas and choices in cross-cultural counseling: The universal versus the culturally distinctive. In P. Pederson, J. Draguns, W. Lonner, & J. Trimble (Eds.), *Counseling cross cultures* (pp. 3–22). Honolulu: University of Hawaii Press.

Dwairy, M. (1998). *Cross-cultural counseling: The Arab-Palestinian case.* Binghamton, NY: Haworth Press.

El Saadawi, N. (1995). Women should reject Islamic gender roles. Interview by G. Lerner. In D. Bender & B. Leone (Eds.), *Islam: Opposing view points* (pp. 80–88). San Diego, CA: Greenhaven Press.

Encyclopaedia Britannica almanac. (2003). Chicago: Encyclopaedia Britannica.

Erikson, E. H. (1959). Identity and the life cycle. In *Psychological issues monographs* (Vol. 1, 1–171). New York: International Universities Press.

Esposito, J. (1982). *Women in Muslim family law.* Syracuse, NY: Syracuse University Press.

Esposito, J. (1991). *Islam and politics* (3rd ed.). Syracuse, NY: Syracuse University Press.

Esposito, J. (1995). Islam: An overview. In J. Esposito (Ed.), *Encyclopedia of the modern Islamic world* (pp. 243–254). New York: Oxford University Press.

Esposito, J. (1996). The Washington Report on Middle East Affairs (November/December 96): Georgetown University holds conference on globalization and Islam. In *Oxford Encyclopedia of the Modern Islamic World* (Vol. 2, pp. 243–254). Oxford: Oxford University Press; Syracuse, NY: Syracuse University Press.

Esposito, J. (1998). *Islam: The straight path* (3rd ed.). New York: Oxford University Press.

Esposito, J. (1999). *The Islamic threat.* Oxford: Oxford University Press.

Esposito, J. (Ed.). (1993). *Islam in Asia: Religion, politics, and society.* New York: Oxford University Press.

Farah, C. (Ed.). (1994). *Islam.* Hauppauge, NY: Barron's.

Farris, C. (1992, October). Even an eight-year-old boy can tell Middle East fact from fiction. *Washington Report on Middle East Affairs,* 40.

Findly, P. (1992, October). A campaign to discredit Islam? Time for American Muslims to wake up. *Washington Report on Middle East Affairs,* 38, 83.

Fisher, M. (Ed.). (1997). *Living religions* (2nd ed.). Englewood Cliffs, NJ: Prentice Hall.

Foley, V. D. (1989). Family therapy. In R. J. Corsini & D. Wedding (Eds.), *Current psychotherapies* (4th ed.). Itasca, IL: Peacock Publishers, Inc.

Folkenberg, J. (1986). Mental health of Southeastern refugees. *ADAMHA News,* 12(1), 10–11.

Fuller, G. (1997, September). The rise of Islam in central Asia. *The World & I.*

Geertz, C. (1968). *Islam observed: Religious development in Morocco and Indonesia.* New Haven, CT: Yale University Press.

Geertz, C. (1973). *The interpretation of cultures.* New York: Basic Books.

Glanz, E. G. (1974). *Guidance foundation, principles and techniques* (2nd ed.). Boston: Allyn & Bacon.

Goldman, A. (1993, 4 May). Thriving amid harmony, a mosque is transformed. *New York Times,* p. A1.

Haddad, Y. (1986). *A century of Islam in America.* Occasional paper no. 4. Washington, DC: The Middle East Institute.

Haddad, Y. (Ed.). (1991). *The Muslims of America.* New York: Oxford University Press.

Haddad, Y. (1998). *The dynamics of islamic identity in North America.* In Y. Haddad & J. Esposito (Eds.), *Muslims on the Americanization path?* Atlanta: Scholars Press.

Haddad, Y., & Esposito, J. (Eds.). (1998). *Muslims on the American path?* Atlanta, GA: Scholars Press.

Haddad, Y., & Lummis, A. (1987). *Islamic values in the United States: A comparative study.* New York: Oxford University Press.

Haley, J. (1967). Marriage therapy. In H. Greenwald (Ed.), *Active psychotherapy.* Chicago: Aldine.

Haneef, S. (1993). *What everyone should know about Islam and Muslims.* Des Plaines, IL: Library of Islam.

Hansen, J., Stevic, R., & Warner, R., Jr. (1982). *Counseling: Theory and process* (3rd ed.). Boston: Allyn & Bacon.

Hedayat-Diba, Z. (2000). Psychotherapy with Muslims. In P. Richards & A. Bergin (Eds.), *Handbook of psychotherapy and religious diversity* (pp. 289–314). Washington, DC: American Psychological Association.

Hills, H., & Strozier, A. (1992). Multicultural training in APA-approved counseling psychology program: A survey. *Professional Psychology Research and Practice*, 23(1), 43–51.

Ibrahim, F. (1991). Contribution of cultural worldview to generic counseling and development. *Journal of Counseling and Development*, 70(1), 13–19.

Jackman, M., & Muha, M. (1984). Education and intergroup attitudes: Moral enlightenment, superficial democratic commitment, or ideological refinement? *American Sociological Review*, 49(6), 751–769.

Jackson, B. (1975). Black identity development: MEFORM. *Journal of Educational Diversity and Innovation*, 2, 19–25.

Jackson, M. (1991). Counseling Arab Americans. In C. Lee & B. Richardson (Eds.), *Multicultural issues in counseling: New approaches to diversity* (pp. 179–206). Alexandria, VA: American Association for Counseling and Development.

Jackson, M. (1995). Multicultural historical perspectives. In J. Ponterotto et al. (Eds.), *Handbook of multicultural counseling*. Thousand Oaks, CA: SAGE Publications.

Jafari, M. (1993). Counseling values and objectives: A comparison of Western and Islamic perspectives. *American Journal of Islamic Social Sciences*, 10(3), 326–339.

Jalali, B. (1996). Iranian families. In M. McGoldrick, J. Giordano, & J. Pearce (Eds.), *Ethnicity and family therapy* (pp. 347–363). New York: Guilford Press.

Jensen, J. P., & Bergin, A. E. (1988). Mental health values of professional therapists: A national interdisciplinary survey. *Professional Psychology: Research and Practice*, 14, 290–297.

Jones, A., & Seagull, A. (1977). Dimensions of the relationship between the black client and white therapist. *American Psychologist*, 32, 850–855.

Juarez, R. (1985). Core issues in psychotherapy with Hispanic child. *Psychotherapy*, 22, 441–448.

Kahn, M. (1998). Muslims and identity politics in America. In Y. Haddad & J. Esposito (Eds.), *Muslims on the Americanization path?* Atlanta, GA: Scholars Press.

Kelly, E., Jr., Aridi, A., & Bakhtiar, L. (1996). Muslims in the United States: An exploratory study of universal and mental health values. *Counseling and Values*, 40, 206–218.

Kobeisy, A. (1997). *Muslim youths in the United States: Potential strength or future enemy*. Riyadh, Saudi Arabia: World Association of Muslim Youths.

Kobeisy, A. (1999a). *The application of Islamic family law in the American judicial system*. Paper presented at the Fifth Annual Symposium of the Institute of Islamic and Arabic Studies of America, Fairfax, VA.

Kobeisy, A. (1999b). The portrait of the Muslim scholar in the United States and the role Muslim communities can play to end bias in American Academic institutions. *American Journal of Islamic Social Sciences*, 16(3), 65–79.

Kosmin, B., & Lachman, S. (1993). *One nation under God: Religion in contemporary American society*. New York: Harmony Books.

Kushner, M. G., & Sher, K. L. (1991). The relation of treatment fearfulness and psychological service utilization: An overview. *Professional Psychology Research and Practice, 22,* 196–203.

Lang, J. (1994). *Struggling to surrender.* Beltsville, MD: Amana Publications.

Lang, J. (1997). *Even angels ask: A journey to Islam in America.* Beltsville, MD: Amana Publications.

Langman, P. (1995). Including Jews in multiculturalism. *Journal of Multicultural Counseling and Development, 23*(4), 222–236.

Lee, C. (1991). Cultural dynamics: Their importance in multicultural counseling. In C. Lee & B. Richardson (Eds.), *Multicultural issues in counseling: New approaches to diversity* (pp. 11–17). Alexandria, VA: American Association for Counseling and Development.

Lee, C., Oh, M.,& Mountcastle, A. (1992). Indigenous models of helping in nonwestern countries: Implications for multicultural counseling. *Journal of Multicultural Counseling and Development, 20,* 3–10.

Lee, E. (1996). American Asian families. In M. McGoldrick, J. Giordano, & J. Pearce (Eds.), *Ethnicity and family therapy* (2nd ed.). New York: Guilford Press.

Lefley, H. P. (1989). Counseling refugees: The North American experience. In P. Pedersen, J. Draguns, W. Lonner, & J. Trimble (Eds.), *Counseling across cultures* (pp. 243–268). Honolulu: University of Hawaii Press.

Lorion, R. P., & Parron, D. L. (1985). Counseling the counter transference: A strategy for treating the untreatable. In P. Pederson (Ed.), *Cross cultural counseling and therapy* (pp. 79–87). Westport, CT: Greenwood Press.

Mahmoud, V. (1996). African American Muslim families. In M. McGoldrick, J. Giordano, & J. Pearce (Eds.), *Ethnicity and family therapy* (pp. 112–128). New York: Guilford Press.

Marquand, R. (1996a, 12 February). Muslims in America: Faith and future. *Christian Science Monitor,* pp. 1 & 10.

Marquand, R. (1996b, 5 February). Muslims in America: Political inroads. *Christian Science Monitor,* pp. 1 & 10.

Marquand, R., & Andoni, L. (1996a, 29 January). Family Islamic values: Simmer in a USA melting pot. *Christian Science Monitor,* pp. 1 & 10.

Marquand, R., & Andoni, L. (1996b, 22 January). Muslims in America: Finding their place. *Christian Science Monitor,* pp. 9–10.

Marshall, L., & Kratz, N. (1988). First impressions: Analog experiment on counselor behavior and gender. *Representative Research in Social Psychology, 18*(1), 41–50.

Mawdudi, A. (1980). *Human rights in Islam.* Leicester, UK: Islamic Foundation.

Mazrui, A. (1991). *Multiculturalism and comparative holocaust: Educational and moral implications.* Annex to the Report of the New York Social Studies Review and Development Committee. Albany: The New York State Education Department.

Melton, J. G. (1993). *Encyclopedia of American Religions* (4th ed.). Detroit: Gale Research.

Miles, J. (1996). *God: A biography.* New York: Vintage Books.

Miller, G. (1999). The development of spiritual focus in counseling and counselor education. *Journal of Counseling and Development, 77*(4), 498–501.

Minchun, S. (1974). *Families and family therapy.* Cambridge, MA: Harvard University Press.

Misumi, D. (1993). Asian American Christian attitudes towards counseling. *Journal of Psychology and Christianity, 12*(3), 214–224.

Mustikhan, A., & Ansari, M. (1998, February). Women's woes under Islam. *The World & I,* 54–59.

Mutahhari, M. (1991). *The rights of women in Islam.* Tehran: WOFIS.

Nasr, Seyyed H. (1981). *Islamic life and thought.* Albany: State University of New York Press.

Nasr, Seyyed H. (1990). *Traditional Islam in the modern world.* London: Kegan Paul International.

New York State Education Department. (1991). *The Report of Social Studies Syllabus Review and Development Committee.* Albany: The New York State Education Department.

The New York Times Almanac. (2002). J. Wright (Ed.). New York: The Times, Penguin.

Noakes, G. (1998). Muslims in the American press. In Y. Haddad & J. Esposito (Eds.), *Muslims on the Americanization path?* Atlanta, GA: Scholars Press.

Nwadiora, E. (1996). Nigerian families. In M. McGoldrick, J. Giordano, & J. Pearce (Eds.), *Ethnicity and family therapy* (2nd ed.). New York: Guilford Press.

Nyang, S. (1991). Convergence and divergence in an emergent community: A study of challenges facing U.S. Muslims. In Y. Haddad (Ed.), *The Muslims of America* (pp. 236–249). New York: Oxford University Press.

Ostling, R. (1988, 23 May). Americans facing toward Mecca. *Time, 49*–50.

Patterson, C. H. (1989). Values in counseling and psychotherapy. *Counseling and Values, 33,* 164–176.

Pedersen, P. (1988). *A handbook for developing multicultural awareness.* Alexandria, VA: American Association for Counseling and Development.

Pedersen, P. (1991). Multiculturalism as a generic approach to counseling. *Journal of Counseling and Development, 70*(1), 6–12.

Pedersen, P., Fukuyama, H., & Heath, A. (1989). Client, counselor, and contextual variables in multicultural counseling. In P. Pedersen, J. Draguns, W. Lonner, & J. Trimble (Eds.), *Counseling across cultures* (pp. 23–52). Honolulu: University of Hawaii Press.

Pomales, J., Claiborn, C. D., & La Formboise, T. D. (1986). Effects of black students' racial identity on perception of white counselors varying in cultural sensitivity. *Journal of Counseling Psychology, 33,* 57–61.

Ponterotto, J., Casas, J., Suzuki, L., & Alexander, C. (Eds.). (1995). *Handbook of multicultural counseling.* Thousand Oaks, CA: SAGE Publications.

Poston, W., Craine, M., & Atkinson, D. (1991). Counselor dissimilarity confrontation, client cultural mistrust, and willingness to self-disclose. *Journal of Multicultural Counseling and Development, 19,* 115–129.

The Post Standard. (1993, 17 February). Scholar: Africans discovered New World, p. D10.

Pugh, R., Ackerman, B. J., McColgan, E. B., & de-Nesguila, P. (1994). Attitudes of adolescents toward adolescent psychiatric treatment. *Journal of Child and Family Studies, 3*(4), 351–363.

Quintana, S., & Bernal, M. (1995). Ethnic minority training in counseling psychology: Comparisons with clinical psychology and proposed standards. *Counseling Psychologist, 23*(1), 102–121.

Rashid, Hakim Muhammed. (1990). *In search of the path: Socialization, education and the African Muslim.* Capitol Hights, MD: Imania Publications.

Reitmeyer, R. (2000, March). Dog gone? From cats to snakes. *Counseling Today*, 1.

Ridley, C. (1995). *Overcoming unintentional racism in counseling and therapy: A prac-titioner's guide to intentional intervention*. Thousand Oaks, CA: SAGE Publi-cations.

Root, M. P. P. (1985). Guidelines for facilitating therapy with Asian American cli-ents. *Psychotherapy, 22*, 349–356.

Rosenthal, D. (1955). Change in some moral values following psychotherapy. *Jour-nal of Counseling Psychology, 19*, 431–436.

Sachedina, A. (1997, September). What is Islam? *The World & I*, 45–49.

Said, E. (1981). *Covering Islam*. New York: Pantheon Books.

Schore, L. (1990). Issues of work, workers, and therapy. *New Directions for Mental Health Services*, (summer), 93–100.

Sharabi, H. (Ed.). (1990). *Theory, politics and the Arab world*. New York: Routledge.

Smith, J. (1997, September). Joining the debate. *The World & I*, 60–67. The Wash-ington Times Corporation.

Smith, J. (1999). Islam and Christendom: Historical, cultural, and religious inter-action from the seventh to the fifteenth centuries. In J. Esposito (Ed.), *The Oxford History of Islam* (pp. 305–346). Oxford University Press, New York.

Spradely, J. P. (1980). *Participant observation*. New York: Holt, Rinehart & Winston.

Sprinthall, N. A. (1971). *Guidance for human growth*. New York: Van Nostrand.

Staff. (1994, May/June). U.S. survey of minority stereotypes shows they are wide-spread. *Fellowship*, 22.

Steinfels, R. (1993, 7 May). Muslims in America: Islam in America has many faces. *New York Times*, pp. A1, A20.

Stivens, M. (1996). *Matrilineal and modernity: Sexual politics and social change in rural Malaysia*. St. Leonards, Australia: Allen & Unwin.

Stone, C. (1991). Estimate of Muslims living in America. In Y. Haddad (Ed.), *The Muslims of America* (pp. 25–36). Oxford: Oxford University Press.

Sue, D. W. (1978). World views and counseling. *Personal and Guidance Journal, 56*, 458–463.

Sue, D. W. (1989). Racial, cultural, identity development among Asian-Americans: Counseling/therapy implications. *AAPA Journal, 13*(1), 80–86.

Sue, D. W., Arredondo, P., & McDavis, R. (1992). Multicultural counseling com-petencies and standards: A call to the profession. *Journal of Counseling and Development, 70*, 477–486.

Sue, S., & Sue, D. W. (1971). Chinese-American personality and mental health. *Amerasia Journal, 1*, 36–49.

Sundberg, N., & Sue, D. (1989). Research and related research hypotheses about effectiveness in intercultural counseling. In P. Pedersen, J. Draguns, W. Lon-ner, & J. Trimble (Eds.), *Counseling across cultures* (pp. 335–370). Honolulu: University of Hawaii Press.

Szivos, S. E., & Griffiths, E. (1990). Group processes involved in coming to terms with mentally retarded identity. *Mental Retardation, 28*(6), 333–341.

Taibi, B. (1991). *Islam and the cultural accommodation of social change*. Boulder, CO: Westview Press.

Tanaka-Matsumi, J., & Higginbotham, H. (1989). Behavioral approaches to coun-seling across cultures. In P. Pedersen, J. Draguns, W. Lonner, & J. Trimble

(Eds.), *Counseling across cultures* (pp. 269–298). Honolulu: University of Hawaii Press.

Thomas, R. (1990). *Counseling and life-span development*. Newbury Park, CA: SAGE Publications.

Tyler, L. (1969). *The work of the counselor* (3rd ed.). New York: Appleton-Century-Crofts.

Tyler, S., Fiske, S., Etcott, N., & Ruderman, A. (1978). Categorical and contextual bases of person memory and stereotyping. *Journal of Personality and Social Psychology, 36*(7), 778–793.

Voll, J. (1991). Islamic issues for Muslims in the United States. In Y. Haddad (Ed.), *The Muslims of America* (pp. 205–216). Oxford: Oxford University Press.

Wadley, S. (1994). *Struggling with destiny in Karimpur, 1924–1984*. Berkeley: University of California Press.

Walsh, W., & Betz, N. (1990). *Tests and assessment*. Englewood Cliffs, NJ: Prentice Hall.

Walther, W. (1995). *Women in Islam, from medieval to modern times*. Princeton, NJ: Markus Weiner Publishers.

Waugh, E., Abu Laban, B., & Qureshi, R. (1991). *The Muslim community in North America*. Alberta: The University of Alberta Press.

Weaver, A., Koenig, H., & Larson, D. (1997, January). Marriage and family therapists and the clergy: A need for clinical collaboration, training, and research. *Journal of Marital and Family Therapy, 23*, 13–25. U.S. American Association for Marriage and Family Therapy.

Webster, D. W., & Fretz, B. R. (1978). Asian American, black and white college students' preferences for help-giving source. *Journal of Counseling Psychology, 25*, 124–130.

Williamson, E. G. (1965). *Vocational counseling*. New York: McGraw-Hill.

The World Almanac and Book of Facts. (2000). New York: World Almanac Books.

Woodward, M. (1995). Popular religion. In J. Esposito (Ed.), *The Oxford encyclopedia of the modern Islamic world* (Vol. 3, pp. 336–338). New York: Oxford University Press.

Wormser, R. (1994). *American Islam: Growing up Muslim in America*. New York: Walker and Company.

Worthington, E. (1989). Religious faith across the life span: Implications for counseling and research. *Counseling Psychologist, 17*, 555–612.

Zahran, H. (1977). *Psychology of growth* (in Arabic). Cairo: A'lam Al-Kitab.

Additional Readings

Abd al'Ati. H. (1975). *Islam in focus*. Indianapolis: American Trust Publications.

Abd al' Ati. H. (1977). *The family structure in Islam*. Indianapolis: American Trust Publications.

Abu-Lughod, L. (1990). Anthropology's Orient: The boundaries of theory on the Arab world. In H. Sharabi (Ed.), *Theory, politics and the Arab world* (pp. 81–131). London: Routledge.

Al-Azmeh, Aziz. (1993). *Islam and modernities*. London: Verso.

Al-Faruqi, I. (1984). *Islam*. Brentwood, MD: International Graphics.

Al-Faruqi, I., & Al-Faruqi, L. (1986). *The cultural atlas of Islam*. New York: Macmillan.

Ali, A. Y. (1990). *The Holy Qur'an: English translation of the meanings and commentary.* Madinah Munawwarah, Saudi Arabia: King Fahd for Mushaf Publications.

Al-Munajjed, M. (1997). *Women in Saudi Arabia today.* New York: St. Martin's Press.

Altorki, S. (1986). *Women in Saudi Arabia.* New York: Columbia University Press.

Assad, M. (1984). *The message of the Qur'an.* Gibraltar, UK: Dar al-Andalus.

Axelson, J. A. (1985). *Counseling and development in a multicultural society.* Monterey, CA: Brooks/Cole.

Blumer, H. (1969). *Symbolic interaction: Perspectives and method.* Englewood Cliffs, NJ: Prentice Hall.

Briggs, D. (1993, 1 May). Mainstream religious leaders loath to accept Islam, leaders say. *Washington Post,* pp. G10–G11.

Clifford, J. (1983). On ethnographic authority. *Reflections, 1*(2), 118–146.

Clifford, J. (1986). Introduction: Partial truths. In J. Clifford & G. Marcus (Eds.), *Writing culture: The poetics and politics of ethnography* (pp. 1–26). Berkeley: University of California Press.

Clifford, J., & Marcus, G. E. (Eds.). (1986). *Writing culture: The poetics and politics of ethnography.* Berkeley: University of California Press.

Donohue, J., & Esposito, J. (Eds.). (1982). *Islam in transition.* Oxford: Oxford University Press.

The Economist. (1994, 6–12 August).

Editor. (1994, July). *American Muslim Journal.*

Esposito, J. (1984). *Islam and politics.* Syracuse, NY: Syracuse University Press.

Gilsenan, M. (1992). *Recognizing Islam: Religion and society in the modern Middle East.* London: I. B. Tauris.

Gordon, S. (1991). *The history and philosophy of social science.* London: Routledge.

Hamid, M. (1981). *Islam and social development* (in Arabic). International Institute for Islamic Thought (IIIT). Jeddah, Saudi Arabia: Manarah Publishing.

Ibn Khaldun. (1976). *The Muqaddimah of Ibn Khaldun: An introduction to history* (F. Rosenthal, Trans.). Princeton, NJ: Bollingen Series.

Hathout, H. (1995). *Reading the Muslim mind.* Indianapolis: American Trust Publications.

Jameelah, M. (1976). *Islam and Western society.* Lahore, Pakistan: Muhammad Yusuf Khan & Sons.

Jameelah, M. (1981). *Islam and orientalism.* Lahore, Pakistan: Muhammad Yusuf Khan & Sons.

Keddie, N., & Baron, B. (Eds.). (1992). *Women in Middle Eastern history.* New Haven, CT: Yale University Press.

Lewis, B. (1988). *The political language of Islam.* Chicago: University of Chicago Press.

Lewis, B. (1993). *Islam and the West.* Oxford: Oxford University Press.

Lewis, B. (Ed.). (1987). *Islam from the Prophet Muhammad to the capture of Constantinople.* New York: Oxford University Press.

Moore, P., & Boyd-Franklin, N. (1996). African American families. In M. McGoldrick, J. Giordano, & J. Pearce (Eds.), *Ethnicity and family therapy* (pp. 66–84). New York: Guilford Press.

Pedersen, P. (1990). The multicultural perspective as a fourth force in counseling. *Journal of Mental Health Counseling, 12,* 93–95.

Petersen, J. A. (1970). *Counseling and values.* Scranton, PA: International Textbook.

Piercy, F., Soekandar, A., & Limansubroto, C. (1996). Indonesian families. In M. McGoldrick, J. Giordano, & J. Pearce (Eds.), *Ethnicity and family therapy* (pp. 316–323). New York: Guilford Press.

Ridely, C. (1989). Racism in counseling as an aversive behavioral process: The universal versus the culturally distinctive. In P. Pederson, J. Draguns, W. Lonner, & J. Trimble (Eds.), *Counseling across cultures* (pp. 55–78). Honolulu: University of Hawaii Press.

Roudi, N. (1988, March). Demographer's page: The demography of Islam. *Population Today*, pp. 6–7.

Said, E. (1979). *Orientalism*. New York: Vintage Books.

Sharabi, H. (1988). *Neopatriarchy*. Oxford: Oxford University Press.

Siddiqui, M. (Ed.). (1994). *Islam: A contemporary perspective*. Chicago: NAAMPS Publications.

Simon, J. (1996). Lebanese families. In M. McGoldrick, J. Giordano, & J. Pearce (Eds.), *Ethnicity and family therapy* (pp. 364–375). New York: Guilford Press.

Sue, D. W. (1981). *Counseling the multiculturally different: Theory and practice*. New York: John Wiley & Sons.

Tibi, B. (1991). *Islam and the cultural accommodation of change*. Oxford: Westview Press.

Triandis, H. (1996). The psychological measurement of cultural syndromes. *American Psychologist, 51*, 407–415.

Voll, J. (1982). *Islam: Continuity and change in the modern world*. Syracuse, NY: Syracuse University Press.

Watt, W. (1961). *Muhammad: Prophet and statesman*. New York: Oxford University Press.

Watt, W. (1966). *A short history of Islam*. Oxford: Oneworld.

Waugh, E. H., Abu Laban, S. M., & Qureshi, R. B. (1991). *Muslim families in North America*. Ontario: University of Alberta Press.

Williams, W., et al. (1991). *Javanese lives: Women and men in modern Indonesian society*. New Brunswick, NJ: Rutgers University Press.

Wright, J. (Ed.). (2002). *The New York Times almanac*. New York: The Times.

Index

Names in bold are clients and counselors referred to in this book

About the Author

AHMED NEZAR KOBEISY is on the faculty at Le Moyne College, State University of New York at Oswego and Hartford Seminary. He is also a counselor and Imam at the Islamic Society of Central New York. Furthermore, he is the Islamic Chaplain at Syracuse University.